MANIFESTATION JOURNAL

YOUR PATH TO DREAMS AND ABUNDANCE

MANIFESTATION JOUNRAL

Your Path to Dreams and Abundance

First Edition

Contents

01.

Introduction

Embarking on the Journey

Unlocking Your Manifestation Power

Welcome to Your Transformative Path — your very own Manifestation Journal, a crafted guide to unlocking your deepest desires and highest aspirations. This isn't just a book; it's a journey and a series of stepping stones towards the life you've envisioned in your quietest moments and your grandest dreams.

If you are not familiar with the law of attraction, consider this a warm welcome into the world of manifestation. The Law of Attraction isn't just a concept; it's an actionable, vibrant force that responds to your thoughts, emotions, and beliefs. It's about shifting from a mindset of scarcity to one of abundance, from a place of doubt to a realm of certainty in your own capabilities.

This journal is more than a guide; it's a dynamic companion on your journey of manifestation. Designed to meet you at your current stage of understanding and evolve with you. This journal is structured to not only introduce the principles of manifestation to the beginners but also to provide deeper, more nuanced insights for those looking to expand their knowledge and understanding. As you grow and progress, this journal celebrates your successes and continues to challenge and inspire you, ensuring that it remains a relevant and supportive tool at every step of your manifestation journey.

Imagine a process so potent that it transforms 'what if' into 'what is.' That's the essence of the Law of Attraction. It's not about battling for every bit of happiness or accomplishment. It's about believing in the magnetic power of your dreams, recognizing they are as much a part of your destiny as you are of theirs.

This journal is an invitation to step into your power, to recognize that your dreams aren't just fleeting wishes or wishful thinking but seeds ready to sprout with the right nourishment. Here, you'll learn to cultivate them with intention, care, and a newfound understanding that the universe is eager to collaborate with you.

You hold in your hands more than pages bound together; you hold possibility, potential, and the promise of a life aligned with your deepest desires. So, let's begin this adventure together, with open hearts and minds ready to manifest the extraordinary.

Turn the page. Your future awaits.

02.

Introduction to the Law of Attraction

Embracing the Power of Your Thoughts

If you're reading this journal, it probably means you already have some idea about the Law of Attraction but might not be sure how to make it work for you, how to apply it effectively, and how to turn your dreams into reality. For those who are relatively new to the concept of the Law of Attraction and manifesting, let this journal serve as your beginner's guide and for those well-acquainted with the Law of Attraction, consider this journal a comprehensive refresher, designed to reinforce and expand your existing knowledge.

The Law of Attraction is based on the belief that we create and manifest in our lives what we focus our thoughts and attention on. Life isn't meant to be a constant struggle or a relentless fight for every penny. You are destined for an incredible life filled with abundance. This abundance is accessible to everyone and starts with believing in your power and recognizing that your dreams are just as eager to materialize as you are to achieve them.

The Law of Attraction operates on the principle that **'like attracts like.'** Think of your mind as a magnet, drawing towards you the experiences that align with your most dominant thoughts and feelings. Understanding and mastering this law is the first step in learning the art of manifestation. The key takeaway here is that we attract into our lives what we consistently think about, whether those thoughts are worries or desires. If you look back at your life and reflect over the past few years, you might see how your current reality aligns with your past thoughts, demonstrating that life doesn't just happen to us. Instead, we are co-creators, actively shaping our lives with our conscious and subconscious thoughts and beliefs.

The Mechanics of Manifestation

Understanding the mechanics of manifestation is crucial in harnessing the power of the Law of Attraction. It's more than just hoping or wishing; it's about bringing your thoughts, emotions, and energy into alignment with what you wish to achieve. This alignment involves a few key elements:

- **Universal Attraction:** Think of the Law of Attraction like gravity – it's always there and it works the same for everyone. Your thoughts and feelings are like magnets; they pull towards you things that match their energy. So, whatever you spend your time thinking and feeling about, whether good or bad, you're likely to see more of it in your life.
- **Thoughts Shape Reality:** Imagine your thoughts as signals you're sending out into the universe. The universe acts like an echo, sending back experiences that match the vibration of your thoughts. That's why thinking positively often leads to good

things happening, while negative thoughts might end up bringing you situations you'd rather not face.

- **Emotional Guidance:** Your emotions are like a personal GPS system. They show you whether you're on the right track to attracting what you want. Feeling happy, excited, or loving means you're in sync with your desires. But if you're often feeling scared, angry, or down, it might be a hint that you need to refocus your thoughts to align better with your goals.

A Universal Force by Many Names

In this journal, as we explore the Law of Attraction, we often talk about a universal force that responds to our intentions and desires. This force can be understood and named in various ways, and throughout the chapters, we might refer to it as the universe, nature, spirit, or even God. It's important for you to connect with a term that feels right for you. Feel free to embrace the term that aligns best with your beliefs and feelings. Your unique relationship with this universal force is what truly empowers your journey in manifesting your desires.

The Journal's Intent: A Force for Good

This journal is created with the intention to use the Law of Attraction as a tool for positive transformation—not just for personal gain but for the greater good. The practices and insights shared here aim to foster peace, non-violence, and goodness. It's a responsibility placed upon you, the reader, to use this knowledge wisely. As you grow in your ability to manifest your desires, you also have the opportunity to positively impact the world around you. Your journey of manifestation can become a journey of contributing to a world where kindness, abundance, and harmony are abundant for all.

The Basic Steps of Manifesting: Desire, Inspired Action, Detachment

The process of manifesting your dreams is rooted in understanding and practicing three fundamental steps: having a burning desire, taking inspired action, and embracing detachment. Let's delve deeper into each of these aspects, using practical examples to illustrate their significance.

- **Burning Desire: The Core of Your Dream** - Your journey starts with a burning desire. It's the intense longing or aspiration that drives you. For instance, if your dream is to find a loving partner, this desire should resonate deeply within you, aligning with your core values and life vision. This desire is your compass, guiding your decisions and actions.

- **Inspired Action: Creating Opportunities** - Inspired action is about making practical, conscious steps towards your goal. It's a common misconception that the Law of Attraction means things will happen without effort. However, inspired action is an integral part of the process. If you're looking to find a partner, simply wishing won't be enough. You might need to explore new social circles, try online dating, or engage in activities where you could meet someone with similar interests. This isn't about doing 'all the work' but about creating opportunities for your desires to manifest. Remember, even the universe needs a helping hand at times.

- **Detachment: Letting Go of the 'How' and 'When'** - Detachment is perhaps the most misunderstood yet crucial step. It involves letting go of the specific outcomes, timelines, and ways your desire might come to fruition. Continuing with the example of finding a partner, detachment means not getting fixated on every possible physical characteristic, or how and when you'll meet them. It's about trusting that what you desire, or something even better, is on its way to you. Detachment isn't about inaction or apathy; it's about maintaining a healthy perspective and not allowing your happiness to hinge on the exact details of how your dream unfolds.

In the context of the Law of Attraction, these steps work harmoniously. Your burning desire sets the intention and direction. Inspired action involves actively creating pathways for your dreams to manifest, aligning your real-world activities with your aspirations. Detachment, on the other hand, is about mental and emotional release from specific outcomes, allowing the universe to work its magic in ways that might surprise you.

Together, these steps form a powerful framework for manifesting. They balance proactive effort with a receptive mindset, creating a dynamic interplay between personal agency and universal orchestration.

03.

Knowledge Recap

Ground Rules of Manifesting

As we embark on the transformative journey of manifesting, it's crucial to understand the foundational principles that guide this process. This chapter serves as a comprehensive guide, designed to demystify and deepen your understanding of manifesting. Whether you're new to these concepts or seeking to refine your skills, we aim to provide clarity and insight, addressing any uncertainties and laying a solid groundwork for your practice.

Manifesting is more than just a technique; it's a way of life. It requires a shift in mindset, a deep understanding of the universal laws, and a commitment to personal growth. As we explore these principles, you'll find that manifesting is not just about achieving personal goals; it's about aligning with your higher purpose, contributing to the world, and realizing your fullest potential.

In this chapter, we'll revisit key concepts of manifesting, ensuring you have a clear and thorough understanding of each element. We'll explore why manifesting is inherently selfless, the importance of your relationship with your dreams, the significance of focusing on 'what' and 'why' rather than 'how' and 'when', the necessity of believing in your worthiness to receive your desires, and the constant nature of manifestation.

This deep dive aims to equip you with the knowledge and confidence to manifest effectively, bringing your desires from the realm of thought into reality. Let's embark on this enlightening journey together, uncovering the profound truths that underpin successful manifesting.

Manifesting is Selfless

Manifesting is a journey that goes far beyond personal gain; it's a profound path of self-discovery and growth. This journey invites deep introspection and honesty about what truly matters in your life. While confronting these inner truths might not always be easy, the process is incredibly rewarding. Gaining clarity about your goals and desires is the first essential step in making them a reality.

This transformative process requires you to shift your mindset, challenging and replacing limiting beliefs with empowering thoughts. When you start believing in your potential and your ability to realize your dreams, you unlock a powerful personal strength that perhaps you didn't know existed.

Manifesting isn't just about achieving your own goals; it's deeply linked to your ability to positively impact others. When you are happy and abundant, you have more resources, energy, and positivity to share with the world. This could take the form of volunteering, donating, or simply being a source of positivity in your everyday life. Your state of fulfillment enables you to give back in ways that are meaningful and impactful.

It's crucial to understand that focusing on your well-being isn't selfish. In fact, true self-care positions you to be a more effective giver. When struggling with your own challenges, your ability to support others is limited. In such a state, your attempts to help may come from a place of obligation or guilt, lacking the genuine intent that truly benefits others. Moreover, if you're not feeling fulfilled and content, there's a risk of projecting your frustrations onto those you aim to help, causing unintended harm.

By pursuing your dreams and achieving your full potential, you do more than fulfill your own desires; you contribute to spreading positivity and upliftment in the world around you. Your happiness and fulfillment have a ripple effect, extending beyond your personal experience and positively affecting those around you.

Living your best life and realizing your dreams inspires others. Your journey shows what's possible and motivates others to seek their own fulfillment and abundance. Through manifesting your aspirations, you become an agent of positive change, affecting not just your life but also the lives of those you touch.

Embrace your manifesting journey with trust and belief in the process. Recognize that you have the power to achieve anything that aligns with your true self. This path isn't just about personal transformation; it's about creating waves of positivity and growth that reach far beyond your individual experience, touching the lives of those around you and contributing to a world where more people can find their own path to happiness and fulfillment.

Your Dreams are a Unique Divine Assignment & Nature Wants You to Achieve Your Dreams

Manifesting your dreams is often misunderstood as being selfish. But this idea is far from the truth. In fact, nature, the universe, God, or whatever higher power you believe in, actually wants you to bring your dreams into fruition as much as you do. These dreams and desires you have aren't just random; they're like a personal mission given to you, and it's your job to follow them.

The universe is like a vast treasure chest of possibilities and support, all designed to help you grow and flourish. When you focus on what makes you truly happy and fulfilled, you're not just thinking about yourself. You're actually moving in sync with the universe's natural flow. This isn't selfishness; it's living in harmony with the way things are meant to be.

It's important to remember that what you want for yourself isn't necessarily what everyone else wants. There's no need to fight over dreams or feel guilty about going after yours. Everyone has their own unique dreams and goals. Figuring out and going after what you truly want is like claiming a gift that's been waiting just for you – it's your personal right.

Your dreams are much more than just daydreams or wishful thinking. They're signs pointing you towards your special role in life. Following your dreams means you're not just chasing personal satisfaction; you're making a meaningful contribution to the world. We all have unique talents and gifts, and chasing your dreams means you're using these special abilities in the best way possible.

By pursuing what you're genuinely passionate about, you're not only making yourself happier – you're also adding something valuable to the world. It's like when you're happy and fulfilled, you naturally make the world around you a better place.

So, embrace your dreams. They're not selfish desires but crucial parts of a bigger picture that includes not just you but the world around you. Your dreams are a call to step into the role you're meant to play, bringing both personal joy and greater good to the world.

Clarity on Desires: Focusing on 'What' and 'Why' Over 'How' and 'When'

Understanding and focusing on your true desires – the 'what' and 'why' – is crucial in the journey of manifestation. This approach encourages you to delve deep into the essence of your dreams, to really grasp what you want and understand why it's important to you. This clarity is what sets the stage for successful manifesting.

The Importance of Knowing 'What' - The 'what' in manifesting is about identifying your true desires. It's not just about vague ideas or fleeting wishes; it's about having a clear, specific vision of what you desire. Whether it's a particular job, a type of relationship, personal achievements, or lifestyle changes, having a definitive goal is key. This clarity in what you want is like setting a destination in a navigation system – it guides all your thoughts and actions in the right direction.

The Power of Understanding 'Why' - The 'why' is about your reasons and motivations. It's the driving force behind your dreams. This could range from seeking personal fulfillment and happiness to wanting to make a positive impact on others. Understanding why you want something adds depth and emotion to your desires, making them more powerful. When your dreams are backed by strong, meaningful reasons, they resonate more deeply with you and, in turn, with the universe.

Letting Go of 'How' and 'When' - Focusing on how your dreams will materialize can limit the universe's ability to work its magic. The universe operates in mysterious and often unexpected ways, providing opportunities and pathways that might never cross your mind. For instance, if you dream of traveling but can't see how you'll afford it, don't be bogged down by this uncertainty. The universe could present unforeseen opportunities that can make this dream a reality.

Similarly, obsessing over the timing of your dreams can lead to frustration and impatience. It's natural to want things to happen quickly, but sometimes the best outcomes take time. Trusting the universe's timing is crucial. It might not align with your schedule, but it often turns out to be the perfect timing in hindsight.

The universe is abundant and filled with endless possibilities. When you let go of the need to control the 'how' and 'when,' you open yourself to a broader range of possibilities for your dreams to come true. Focus on your 'what' and 'why,' immerse yourself in these desires, and then allow the universe to take care of the rest. Believe that your dreams are not only possible, they're already in the making. Your role is to set the intention clearly and then step back, allowing the universe to orchestrate the perfect unfolding of your dreams.

Belief in Deserving Your Desires: Embracing Your Worth

In the realm of manifesting, one fundamental truth stands out: 'you don't just get what you want in life; you get what you believe you deserve'. This belief in your own worthiness is a vital component of manifesting your dreams. Let's explore how to cultivate this belief and overcome any limiting beliefs that may be blocking your path to abundance.

- **The Essence of Believing You Deserve Your Dreams** - Often, a significant obstacle in manifesting is the deep-seated belief that you are not worthy of the things you desire. For instance, you might aspire to be wealthy, but if deep inside there's a voice telling you that you're not worthy of financial abundance, this belief will act as a barrier. These are your **limiting beliefs** – the inner narratives that undermine your dreams and make you question your worthiness.

- **Your Dreams are Your Personal Assignment** - It's essential to understand that your desires are not just fleeting whims. They are an integral part of your destiny, divinely inspired and deeply connected to your unique journey in life. They're there for a reason, and they're aligned with your true purpose. When you desire something, it's a sign that it's part of your path, a piece of your puzzle that the universe is waiting to place.

- **Cultivating a Positive Relationship with Your Dreams** - Consider your dreams as entities you're in a relationship with. This means engaging with them in a loving, nurturing manner. If your dream is to find love, for instance, think of this dream as a partner. Anticipate its arrival with joy, treat it with respect, and give it the attention it deserves. This approach creates a bond between you and your dream, making it more likely to manifest.

- **Overcoming Doubts and Fears** - Limiting beliefs about worthiness often arise from past experiences or external opinions. To combat these, it's essential to recognize and confront them. Understand why they exist and challenge them. Replacing them with positive affirmations and beliefs about your worthiness is crucial. Affirm to yourself that you deserve abundance, joy, and fulfillment in every aspect of your life.

- **Embrace Your Right to Fulfillment** - Realize that experiencing joy, abundance, and a fulfilling life is your birthright. You're not here merely to endure struggles and hardships. You are here to thrive, to enjoy life to the fullest, and to fulfill your potential. This mindset shift – from seeing your desires as distant dreams to acknowledging them as deserving realities – is a powerful step in your manifestation journey.

The Power of Gratitude in Manifestation

Gratitude, a transformative force in the practice of manifesting, can be a challenging mindset to cultivate, especially if we grew up in environments where scarcity and unfairness were prevalent. This background often conditions us to focus more on what we lack rather than the abundance that surrounds us. However, shifting our perspective to one of gratitude is not only possible but also deeply rewarding.

In a world that often emphasizes what we don't have, taking time to appreciate the small blessings can feel like an uphill battle. We're trained to strive for more, to see the glass as half empty, and to focus on unmet desires. But the essence of gratitude lies in reversing this view, in recognizing and cherishing what we do have, however small or insignificant it might seem.

Gratitude acts like a magnet for positive experiences. By acknowledging and appreciating the simple pleasures and successes in our lives, we align our energy with abundance and positivity. This alignment attracts more favorable circumstances and opportunities. The universe, in turn, responds to this vibration of gratitude, making it more likely for us to receive even more blessings.

The journey to embracing gratitude starts with acknowledging the small miracles that are often overlooked – a kind word, a beautiful scene, a moment of peace. Recognizing these moments is crucial, as it helps to attract more such positive experiences. It roots us in the present and reveals the hidden abundance in our daily lives.

Cultivating gratitude is about changing our default setting from scarcity to abundance. It involves a conscious decision to focus on the positives, no matter how small. It's about finding that one thing to be thankful for, even on the toughest days. Whether it's a friend's support, a comfortable home, or simply being alive, there's always something to appreciate.

The practice of gratitude is a powerful tool in manifesting our desires. It's not just being thankful for what we have; it's also preparing the ground for what we wish to attract. By expressing gratitude, we open ourselves up to receiving more, setting the stage for the universe to bring our dreams to fruition.

Nature responds to those who appreciate their blessings. When we practice gratitude, we harmonize with the natural flow of giving and receiving. This harmony is a fundamental aspect of manifesting, where our appreciation for the present paves the way for future abundance.

By embracing gratitude, we transform our perception. We begin to see life not as a series of deficiencies but as a canvas rich with possibility and blessings. This shift begins with a simple act of acknowledging and appreciating what we have, no matter how small, and leads us on a path filled with wonder, contentment, and abundance.

Navigating 'Manifestation Anxiety': Focusing on Positive Outcomes

The journey of manifesting your desires can sometimes be accompanied by a state of anxiety, often stemming from the fear of negative outcomes. This phenomenon, which we can term as 'manifestation anxiety' or 'fearful manifesting,' is a common hurdle. It's crucial to navigate through this by focusing on positive outcomes and maintaining an optimistic mindset.

Manifestation anxiety arises when there's a deep-seated fear that your efforts to manifest will lead to negative consequences, or that you won't achieve your desired outcomes. This anxiety can be rooted in past disappointments, a lack of self-belief, or an overarching fear of failure. It's a state where worry overrides hope, casting a shadow over the entire process of manifesting.

To counteract manifestation anxiety, it's important to consciously shift your focus towards positive outcomes. This means actively visualizing success, joy, and fulfillment, rather than dwelling on what could go wrong. It's about trusting the process and believing in the positive possibilities that the future holds.

Strategies to Overcome Fearful Manifesting:

- **Positive Affirmations:** Affirmations are positive, empowering statements that can help shift your mindset from fear to positivity. Repeating phrases like "I am in harmonious alignment with my dreams, effortlessly attracting abundance and joy" or "I am deserving of positive outcomes" reinforces your belief in positive outcomes. It's a way of conditioning your mind to focus on success and abundance, rather than fear and scarcity.

- **Mindfulness and Meditation:** Regular mindfulness practices and meditation can significantly reduce anxiety and fear about future outcomes. By focusing on the present moment, you distance yourself from worries about the future. Meditation helps you find inner calm and clarity, making it easier to approach your manifesting journey with a balanced mindset.

- **Reflect on Past Successes:** Recalling instances where your efforts have previously led to positive outcomes can be very reassuring. It's a way of reminding yourself that success is possible and that you have the ability to manifest your desires. This reflection can be a powerful motivator and confidence booster on your manifestation journey.

- **Journaling:** Writing down your fears and concerns can provide a clear perspective on what's holding you back. Transforming these fears into positive statements in your journal can help in reprogramming your thought patterns. Journaling is also a cathartic exercise that allows you to release and understand your fears, making them less intimidating.

- **Seek Support:** Talking to someone who understands your journey – whether it's a friend, mentor, or a professional – can provide invaluable support. They can offer a new perspective, encouragement, and advice on how to navigate through your fears. This external support can be a crucial element in overcoming blocks in your manifestation process.

- **Celebrate Small Wins:** Recognizing and celebrating even the smallest achievements on your journey towards manifesting your dreams can create a positive feedback loop. It helps build confidence and keeps you motivated. Celebrating these wins can shift your focus from what you haven't achieved yet to the progress you are making.

It's important to maintain a balanced perspective throughout your manifesting journey. Recognize that while outcomes may not always align exactly with your initial vision, each step you take is an integral part of your personal growth and learning process. Manifestation is much more than just achieving a specific end result; it's a journey that involves your entire personal development.

By consciously shifting your focus from fear and anxiety to positivity and optimism, you actively transform the energy you invest in the manifesting process. Remember, the thoughts and emotions you nurture play a pivotal role in shaping your reality. Embracing a mindset of positivity and growth not only enhances your manifestation abilities but also enriches your overall life experience.

Trust in the process of manifestation, and be open to the myriad of wonderful possibilities that life has to offer. Each moment is an opportunity for growth, and every challenge is a stepping stone to greater understanding and achievement. Embrace this journey with a heart full of gratitude and eyes open to the endless potential within you and around you.

Constant Manifestation: It's Happening All the Time

Realizing that manifestation is a continuous process, not just an occasional practice, is vital. It's not something that can be switched on and off. Every moment, consciously or unconsciously, our thoughts and focus are shaping our reality. It's a profound concept: the energy we put out into the world is always shaping our experiences.

Pause and think about how this has played out in your own life. Reflect on those times when you were worried about finances and how, almost predictably, unexpected expenses emerged. Or those instances when your concern about being late for an appointment actually led to unforeseen delays.

These aren't mere coincidences; they are manifestations of where you directed your energy and attention. It's a clear indication that our thoughts, whether positive or negative, have a tangible impact on our lives. This realization can be a bit overwhelming, but it's also empowering. It means that by shifting our focus, we can influence the direction of our lives.

Shifting our attention to positive thoughts and outcomes is more than just an exercise in optimism; it's a powerful tool for change. By concentrating on what brings us joy, hope, and gratitude, we start attracting more of those positive experiences. It's not about ignoring life's challenges; it's about choosing to focus more on the potential for good in our lives.

This shift in focus doesn't mean that everything you desire will materialize instantly. However, it does mean that your journey through life can be more enjoyable and fulfilling. By choosing to focus on the brighter side, even if the Law of Attraction feels like a far-off concept, your day-to-day life becomes richer and more positive.

Remember, we're constantly manifesting, regardless of whether we do it consciously or not. By actively directing our focus towards the positive aspects of life, we guide this perpetual manifestation towards a more joyful and abundant existence. It's a choice to live with optimism and to embrace the possibility of a better, happier life.

Understanding Your Inner Dialogue: The Key to Manifestation

The journey to effective manifestation begins with understanding your inner dialogue. The words and thoughts you entertain throughout your day - in the morning, at work, during meals, and in social interactions - shape your reality. It's crucial to be conscious of these thoughts, as they are the seeds from which your life grows.

We often underestimate the power of our everyday thoughts, but they are the foundation of manifestation. It's not just about what we consciously wish for; it's about the underlying beliefs and narratives that run through our minds constantly. These thoughts, whether they're filled with hope or fear, are what we eventually see reflected in our lives.

Ask yourself, what do you usually think about during your day? Are your thoughts dominated by worries, doubts, and worst-case scenarios? Or do you find moments of hope, gratitude, and anticipation of good things? Your predominant thoughts are not just passive observations; they are actively creating your future.

Manifestation is not just about deciding to be happy or putting on a smile on your face. It's about truly understanding that your thoughts have a direct impact on your life. This realization can be both empowering and intimidating. To harness this power effectively, you must first acknowledge and understand your thought patterns.

Breaking the pattern requires introspection and honesty. It means identifying the source of your limiting beliefs, understanding how they've shaped your life, and then consciously working to change them. This process is about achieving spiritual, emotional, and physical integrity. It's about aligning what you think, how you feel, and what you do, to create a harmonious and productive life.

We are all products of our upbringing and the environments we've been exposed to. These experiences have shaped our thought patterns, which in turn shape our reality. To change our lives, we must be willing to delve into these patterns, understand them, and then actively work to create new, more empowering narratives.

The journey of manifestation is a cycle of thought, feeling, and action. By understanding this cycle and learning to control it, you can start to manifest the life you desire. It's about recognizing the power of your thoughts and using them to create a life that's not just a reaction to your circumstances, but a conscious, deliberate creation of your desires.

Deepening the Understanding of Manifesting Steps: Desire, Inspired Action, Detachment

In Chapter 2, we introduced the essential steps of manifesting: Desire, Inspired Action, and Detachment. The process of manifesting your dreams is rooted in understanding and practicing three fundamental steps which are like ingredients in a recipe, each essential and complementing the other. Now, let's delve deeper into each element, exploring their complexities and interconnections using a practical example to illustrate their significance to enhance your manifesting journey.

1. *Burning Desire: The Foundation of Your Dream*

The starting point of any manifestation journey is a burning desire. This is not just any wish or fleeting thought; it's a deep, passionate longing that aligns with your core values and aspirations. It's the kind of desire that feels like a fire within, driving you forward and illuminating your path.

Take the example of wanting to find a loving partner. This shouldn't be a superficial wish based on societal expectations or momentary loneliness. Instead, it should resonate with your deepest yearnings for companionship, love, and shared experiences. It's about knowing what you genuinely want in a partner and why it's important to you.

This burning desire acts as your guiding star. It shapes your choices, influences your actions, and sets the tone for your manifestation journey.

It's the force that keeps you motivated even when the path gets challenging. It's not just about wanting something; it's about feeling that desire so intensely that it becomes a part of who you are and what you are destined to achieve.

Understanding and acknowledging this desire is crucial. It requires introspection and honesty with oneself. It's about asking the deeper questions: Why do I want this? How does this align with my life's purpose? What will achieving this bring into my life? When your desire is clear, powerful, and aligned with your true self, it becomes a potent force in the manifestation process.

2. *Inspired Action: The Practical Side of Manifestation*

A common area of confusion in understanding the Law of Attraction is the role of action. Many believe that desires will materialize with thought alone, but the concept of inspired action plays a pivotal role. This isn't about hard labor or relentless effort; it's about making mindful, practical steps towards your goals.

Let's continue with the example of manifesting a romantic partner. Merely wishing for a partner is unlikely to be effective. Inspired action in this context could mean expanding your social network, trying online dating, or participating in activities that align with your interests. It's about creating environments and opportunities where your desire can take shape.

This approach isn't about taking on the entire burden of making things happen. Rather, it's about collaborating with the universe. It's about putting yourself in situations where your desires have a chance to meet reality. It's not contradicting the Law of Attraction; it's complementing it.

Engaging in inspired action is like sending a clear, affirmative message to the universe: you're ready and open to receive. It's about taking those intuitive nudges and turning them into tangible steps. Remember, the universe works through us, not just for us. By taking inspired action, you're not just wishing for a change; you're actively participating in its manifestation.

3. *Detachment: Letting Go of the 'How' and 'When'*

Detachment is a critical, yet often misunderstood, element in the manifesting process. It's about releasing the tight grip on the specific outcomes, the exact timelines, and the particular methods through which your desires will materialize. This step is crucial for aligning with the fluid nature of the universe and its countless ways of fulfilling your aspirations.

Let's revisit the example of seeking a loving partner. Detachment in this context means not obsessing over how, when, or where you'll meet this person. It's about releasing the need for control over every detail of this process. Instead, it involves trusting that your desire will manifest in the best way and at the perfect time. It's about believing that what you seek is seeking you, and it could arrive in unexpected, yet perfectly aligned ways.

Detachment is not synonymous with indifference or passivity. It doesn't mean you stop caring about your goal or cease to take meaningful actions towards it. Rather, it's about cultivating a mindset where your inner peace and happiness are not solely dependent on the exact unfolding of your dreams. It's about having faith that the universe has your back and that your desires will be fulfilled, perhaps in ways that are even better than you could have imagined.

In the context of the Law of Attraction, these steps work harmoniously. Your burning desire sets the intention and direction. Inspired action involves actively creating pathways for your dreams to manifest, aligning your real-world activities with your aspirations. Detachment, on the other hand, is about mental and emotional release from specific outcomes, allowing the universe to work its magic in ways that might surprise you.

Together, these steps form a powerful framework for manifesting. They balance proactive effort with a receptive mindset, creating a dynamic interplay between personal agency and universal orchestration.

Manifesting from the Right Brain Hemisphere: A Journey of Creativity and Emotion

Embarking on the path of manifesting, it's essential to understand the distinct roles played by the hemispheres of our brain. Our daily reliance on the left brain for logical thinking, planning, and language is undeniable. It orchestrates much of our lives, guiding us through routine tasks and complex decision-making processes. Yet, the true essence and transformative power of manifesting are intricately linked to the capabilities of our right brain hemisphere.

This segment of our brain is a fountain of creativity, emotions, and intuition. It's here, in the right brain, where we can dive deep into our subconscious mind. This dive is not just an exploration but an unlocking of new, expansive possibilities and innovative solutions, critical to the manifesting process. The left brain, while essential for analytical and logical operations, can often be a source of self-imposed barriers such as negative self-talk and limiting beliefs. These mental constraints can significantly impede our manifesting efforts by getting us stuck in the details of 'how' and 'why,' instead of nurturing a belief in the reality of our desires.

The art of manifesting requires a paradigm shift—a move away from the logical rigidity of the how and why, towards embracing the emotional and intuitive aspects of our desires. The right brain emerges as a guiding light in this shift, allowing us to center our attention on the feelings and emotions that our aspirations stir within us. This focus is not on the procedural elements of their actualization but on their emotional resonance. Such an alignment with the universe's energy streamlines the journey of attracting what we earnestly seek.

Visualization stands out as a potent instrument in this endeavor, and it's an innate strength of the right brain. Visualization in manifesting goes beyond just casual daydreaming. It's an active, deliberate process of constructing a detailed, sensory-rich mental depiction of our desired outcomes. This process involves engaging all our senses to paint a vibrant and detailed picture within our mindscape. The realism and intensity of this mental imagery play a pivotal role in amplifying the effectiveness of our manifestation efforts. The more tangible and immersive our visualization, the more potent its impact on our journey to bring our dreams to life.

Activating our right brain is key to unlocking our manifestation potential. Here are some ways to engage this part of your brain:

1. **Meditation:** Embracing mindfulness and visualization meditations is a powerful way to calm the analytical chatter of the left brain, paving the way for the intuitive wisdom of the right brain to

surface. This form of meditation fosters a deep connection with our inner self, enhancing our manifestation capabilities.

2. **Creative Activities:** Engaging in artistic endeavors such as painting, drawing, music, and dance goes beyond mere leisure. These activities are portals that open us to the rich, creative essence of our right brain. They foster an environment where intuition and creativity can flourish, essential elements in the manifesting process.

3. **Nature Engagement:** Immersing oneself in the tranquility of nature is like a tonic for the right brain. It helps us reconnect with our deeper selves, away from the hustle of everyday life. This reconnection is pivotal in aligning our desires with the natural flow of the universe.

4. **Journaling:** More than just penning down thoughts, journaling is a profound method to explore our deepest aspirations. It harnesses the creative energy of the right brain, helping us to visualize and articulate our dreams and goals with clarity.

5. **Affirmations:** Utilizing affirmations filled with positive emotions can reorient our brain towards our manifestation goals. These affirmations, when repeated with conviction, can reprogram our thought patterns to be more aligned with our aspirations.

6. **Breathing Techniques:** Simple yet effective, breathing exercises such as inhaling through the left nostril can activate the right brain. This activation enhances our creative and intuitive faculties, integral components of successful manifestation.

Incorporating these practices into your daily life can have a transformative effect on your manifestation journey. By engaging the right brain, you do more than just enhance your creative and intuitive skills; you align yourself with the universe's creative essence. This alignment is the key to transforming manifestation from a hopeful wish into a tangible, achievable reality.

Fun and Play in Manifesting: Overcoming Trauma and Limiting Beliefs

Manifesting your desires doesn't have to be a hard, boring or a difficult process. In fact, incorporating elements of fun and play can be incredibly powerful, especially when it comes to overcoming trauma and limiting beliefs. These lighter approaches can help break down the barriers formed by past experiences and negative thought patterns, making room for more positive and fulfilling manifestations.

Fun and play shift your energy from the seriousness and often the stress associated with achieving goals. This shift is vital, especially for those who have experienced trauma or are burdened by deep-seated limiting beliefs. Trauma can lead to a mindset where life is viewed through a lens of survival and hardship, making it difficult to believe in the possibility of joy, abundance, and ease. Playfulness introduces a sense of lightness and possibility, gradually changing this perspective.

Engaging in activities that bring you joy, laughter, and a sense of light-heartedness is essential. It could be anything from dancing to your favorite song, spending time in nature, playing a sport you love, or even engaging in creative pursuits like painting or writing. These activities don't just provide temporary relief or distraction; they help rewire your brain to associate positive emotions with your manifesting journey.

Limiting beliefs, often rooted in past traumas or negative experiences, can act as significant roadblocks in your manifesting journey. Integrating fun and play helps challenge these beliefs by introducing new narratives. For instance, if you've always believed that success comes from struggle and hardship, engaging in enjoyable and playful activities while working towards your goals can help shift this belief. It demonstrates that achievement and pleasure can coexist, breaking the association between success and suffering.

Visualization is a key component of manifesting, and adding an element of fun to this practice can enhance its effectiveness. Imagine your goals and desires, but this time, infuse these visualizations with joyous scenarios, laughter, and a sense of ease. This approach not only makes the process more enjoyable but also imprints the idea of your dreams manifesting in a joyful and stress-free manner.

Lastly, cultivating a playful mindset in your daily life can have profound effects. It's about looking at life's challenges with a sense of curiosity and openness, rather than dread or fear. This mindset encourages you to find joy in the journey of manifesting, making the process as rewarding as the outcome.

Incorporating fun and play in your manifesting journey is not just a strategy; it's a transformative approach that can lead to profound healing and more effective manifestation. It's about rewriting the script of your life from one of trauma and limitation to one of joy, possibility, and abundance.

04.

Challenges and Solutions in Manifestation

Navigating Your Manifestation Path

Welcome to a crucial part of your manifestation journey – addressing challenges and finding solutions. While navigating your manifestation path, you'll undoubtedly face various challenges. These stumbling blocks can sometimes make us doubt the process or even our own abilities. However, understanding and overcoming these challenges is a vital part of our growth and success in manifesting.

In this section, we'll explore some of the biggest pitfalls people face in their manifestation journey. More importantly, we'll provide practical solutions and strategies to navigate these challenges effectively. Whether you're a beginner or have been practicing the Law of Attraction for a while, this chapter will offer insights to refine your manifestation process and achieve greater success.

1. Lack of clarity

One of the most common hurdles in the journey of manifestation is not knowing exactly what you want. This lack of clarity can be a major obstacle in bringing your dreams to fruition. If you're unsure about your true desires, it's like trying to hit a target that you can't see. This often leads to a scattered approach in manifestation, where your energy and focus are diluted because you're not directing them towards a specific goal.

Clarity is essential in the Law of Attraction because it acts as a guiding force for your thoughts and energy. When you know exactly what you want, you can focus your intentions and emotions towards that goal, making your manifestation efforts more powerful and directed.

The journey to clarity involves introspection and sometimes, a bit of trial and error. Here's how you can gain clarity on what you truly desire:

- **Take Time for Self-Reflection:** Dedicate time to think deeply about what you genuinely want in life. It's important to distinguish between what you think you should want (often influenced by others' opinions and societal expectations) and what you truly desire.
- **Journal Your Thoughts and Dreams:** Writing down your thoughts can be a powerful way to process them and gain clarity. It can help you to uncover your true aspirations and understand what genuinely excites and motivates you.
- **Experiment with Different Goals:** Sometimes, you need to try different things to understand what resonates with you. Don't be afraid to explore various interests and passions.

- **Create a Vision Board**: A vision board can be a helpful tool in gaining clarity. By creating a visual representation of your desires, you can better understand and focus on what you truly want.
- **Prioritize Your Desires:** It's okay to have multiple goals, but try to identify which ones are most important to you right now. Focusing on a few key desires can make your manifestation efforts more effective.

Remember, gaining clarity might not be immediate. It's a process that requires patience and self-exploration. In the upcoming chapters, we will revisit this topic and provide exercises to help you further refine your goals and desires. By gaining clarity, you'll be better equipped to focus your manifestation efforts and bring your dreams into reality.

2. Navigating the 'How' of Your Dreams

A common pitfall in the process of manifesting is getting too caught up in figuring out how your dreams will come to fruition. This challenge is closely linked to the concept of detachment, where letting go of the 'how' and 'when' is crucial for successful manifestation.

Many people believe that they need to have a detailed plan for how their dreams will manifest. This belief can lead to unnecessary stress and anxiety, as it's virtually impossible to foresee every step of the manifestation process. It's important to remember that the Law of Attraction isn't about having all the answers upfront. Instead, it's about trusting the universe and being open to the journey, even when the path isn't fully clear.

To overcome this challenge, embrace the unknown and trust that the universe will guide you towards your desires. Here's how to navigate this aspect of manifestation:

- **Let Go of the Need for Control:** Release the need to control every aspect of how your dream will manifest. This doesn't mean you won't play a role in making it happen, but rather that you're open to different possibilities and paths.
- **Trust the Process:** Have faith in the process of manifestation. Believe that the universe has a way of bringing your desires to you in ways that you might not have planned or expected.
- **Stay Open to Opportunities:** Be receptive to opportunities and signs that come your way. Sometimes, the universe presents us with unexpected avenues to our dreams.
- **Take Inspired Action:** When you feel a strong intuitive pull to take a specific action, follow it. This is the universe nudging you towards your goal. Remember, inspired action often feels right and comes with a sense of excitement or curiosity.
- **Remember, It's About Possibility, Not Probability:** Your dreams do not need to feel probable or logical, but they need to feel like they are possible to you. Allow yourself to dream big and trust that what you desire can indeed become your reality.

In summary, don't let the uncertainty of 'how' your dreams will manifest deter you. It's a natural part of the manifestation journey. By letting go of the need to know every detail and trusting in the universe's guidance, you align yourself more closely with the flow of abundance and opportunity.

Remember, the universe works in mysterious ways, often bringing our dreams to life in ways we could never have planned.

3. Tackling the Feeling of Unworthiness

When you embark on the journey of manifesting your dreams, a common internal obstacle you might encounter is the feeling of unworthiness. This hurdle can be daunting, but it's essential to understand and internalize that you are inherently deserving of your dreams and aspirations.

Feeling Unworthy? Here's Why You're More Than Enough

1. **You Are Worthy by Nature**: Remember, the very ability to dream and desire is a testament to your worthiness. The universe, or nature, wouldn't plant these seeds of dreams in you if they weren't meant to grow and flourish. Your dreams are more than fleeting wishes; they are indicators, guiding you towards what you're capable of achieving. They are intertwined with your life's purpose, making you inherently worthy of realizing them.

2. **Ego's Shadow and Its Impact**: The feeling of unworthiness is often the echo of our ego. The ego is good at clinging to what is familiar, fearing change, and defending the known against the unknown. These feelings of unworthiness are the ego's mechanisms to maintain the status quo. Recognizing that these feelings are merely your ego's protective responses allows you to see beyond them and embrace your true potential. It's about understanding that your ego's perception of safety in the familiar is often a barrier to your growth and fulfillment.

3. **Looking Beyond Logic**: Our logical mind, primarily operating from the left brain hemisphere, is crucial for analytical thinking but can be limiting in the context of manifesting dreams. It often attempts to rationalize our aspirations within the boundaries of our past experiences and what it deems logical. Overcoming the feeling of unworthiness involves moving beyond these logical confines, understanding that the realization of your dreams exists beyond the realm of past experiences or logical reasoning. Dreams often reside in the creative and intuitive right hemisphere, a space where possibility and creativity override logical constraints.

In essence, overcoming the feeling of unworthiness involves recognizing your natural entitlement to dream and aspire. It's about understanding that your dreams are an integral part of your existence and that you are more than capable of making them a reality. By acknowledging and embracing your natural right to happiness and success, you open the door to realizing your dreams and living the life you truly desire. Remember, your dreams are seeking you out as much as you are reaching for them, and overcoming the feeling of unworthiness is a crucial step towards manifesting them into reality.

4. Your Desires Are Not Selfish

In the pursuit of manifesting our dreams, especially those around wealth and personal achievements, a sneaky thought often creeps in: 'Is this just selfish?' It's a question worth addressing, but not by reinforcing guilt. Instead, let's reframe our perspective. Your desires, no matter how grand or personal, are not mere whims. They are, in many ways, your soul's language, communicating what it needs to thrive and contribute effectively to the world.

When these aspirations surface, they bring with them a promise – not just of personal fulfillment but of expanded potential to do good. Wealth, success, or achievement, when aligned with your core values, can become tools for broader impact. They enable you to support causes dear to your heart, extend generosity to others, and create positive ripples in your community and beyond.

The key lies in acknowledging that your individual growth and societal contribution are not mutually exclusive. They are intertwined. By nurturing your dreams, you're not taking away from the world; rather, you're preparing yourself to give back in more significant, meaningful ways. Your journey towards your desires is not a solo venture but a part of a greater vision where your success adds color and depth to the collective picture.

So, as you walk this path of manifestation, remember: your dreams are not just for you. They are seeds with the potential to grow into something that benefits many. Embracing this truth allows you to pursue your goals with a heart free of guilt, and a spirit motivated by the potential of positive transformation.

5. Addressing the fear of "What If I fail"?

Embracing your dreams often brings you face-to-face with an all-too-familiar fear: "What if I fail?" It's an echo of your ego, acting like a cautious guardian, constantly reminding you to avoid potential disappointment. Earlier in the chapter, we acknowledged the ego's role in trying to protect us and keep the status quo, but it's also important to understand how to move beyond its limitations.

The ego's warnings are like a safety net, designed to keep you from experiencing pain or failure. It's like having an overly cautious friend who's always advising you to play it safe. This friend means well, but their overprotectiveness can prevent you from taking the leaps necessary to realize your true potential.

However, growth and comfort rarely coexist. To manifest your dreams, you need to step out of your comfort zone, and that means acknowledging the ego's concerns, thanking it for its caution, and then gently pushing it aside. It's about realizing that the fear of failure is a natural part of the journey, not an endpoint.

Let's shift our perspective on failure. Rather than seeing it as a setback or a reason to stop trying, view it as an essential part of your growth. Each misstep is an opportunity to learn, refine your approach, and come back stronger. Remember, the most successful people in history have faced failures and used them as stepping stones to greatness.

By consciously choosing to move past the ego's fear of failure, you open yourself up to a world of possibilities. You allow yourself to dream bigger, take bolder steps, and truly align with your desires. This isn't about disregarding caution entirely but about finding a balance where you can listen to your inner wisdom without being paralyzed by fear.

6. Breaking Free from the 'I Will Be Happy When' Syndrome

When it comes to manifesting, where your mind is at right now makes a huge difference. If you're always thinking, "I'll be happy when I get this or that," it's like you're telling yourself you can't be happy now. That mindset keeps you stuck in a place where you're always waiting for something to make you happy, instead of finding happiness in your life as it is today.

It's really common to think that happiness will come with the next big thing – a new job, a relationship, or any dream you're chasing. But the truth is, if you're always looking ahead for happiness, you might miss the joy that's right in front of you. This doesn't mean you should stop dreaming or working towards your goals. It's about balancing those dreams with being okay and happy with where you are right now.

When you're constantly focused on what you don't have yet, it can make you feel desperate and anxious. This kind of energy can actually push what you want further away. It's like holding on too tight – sometimes, you just need to relax your grip a bit to let things happen.

So, here's the deal: start believing that you deserve to be happy right now, not just in some future where everything's perfect. You don't have to wait for your dreams to come true to start enjoying life. It's about finding little things to be happy about every day, even while you're working towards something bigger.

Shifting from thinking about what's missing to appreciating what you have changes the whole game. It's not about giving up on your dreams; it's about not letting those dreams take away from the happiness you can have right now. Your dreams are important, but so is your happiness today. By finding that balance, you open yourself up to more good things coming your way. Remember, it's not just about chasing happiness in the future – it's also about grabbing onto the happiness that's already around you.

7. Overcoming Victim Mentality

A big obstacle in manifesting your dreams can be a victim mentality – when you believe that you're just not meant for success or happiness. It's like thinking, "Good stuff never happens to people like me." This kind of mindset is really limiting because it's like you're programming yourself to expect failure or disappointment.

When you're stuck in this way of thinking, it's almost like you're telling the universe that you don't believe good things can happen to you. And the universe tends to mirror back what you put out there. So, if you're constantly thinking about how things won't work out, you might just end up proving yourself right, not because you're doomed, but because you're not open to seeing and grabbing the opportunities that come your way.

Shifting out of a victim mentality is about changing your narrative. It's about challenging those negative beliefs and replacing them with thoughts that empower you. For example, instead of thinking, "I never get what I want," try thinking, "I am open to new opportunities and successes." It's about recognizing that good things can and do happen to you.

This shift in mindset doesn't mean you'll never face challenges or setbacks – those are part of everyone's life. But instead of seeing them as confirmations that you're doomed to fail, see them as part of the journey to success. Each challenge is a chance to learn, grow, and get closer to your goals.

Remember, the way you talk to yourself matters. Try to catch yourself when you start thinking in a victim mindset and gently guide your thoughts towards more empowering beliefs. It's about moving from a place of helplessness to a mindset where you're the active creator of your life. When you open yourself up to the belief that good things can happen to you, you start to change your outlook, your actions, and ultimately, your reality.

8. Start Small, Dream Big

When it comes to manifesting, there's a common hurdle: starting too big. It's fantastic to have big dreams, but sometimes, when our goals seem too large or too far away, it can be hard to believe in their attainability. This lack of belief can create resistance and doubt, making the whole process feel overwhelming.

The key here is to start with smaller goals – ones that feel achievable. This doesn't mean you're limiting your dreams; it means you're building your manifesting muscles. Think of it like training for a marathon. You wouldn't start by running 26 miles on your first day. You'd start small, gradually building up your stamina and confidence.

This journal is designed to guide you through this process. By initially focusing on manifesting smaller, more attainable goals, you'll learn the ropes of how manifestation works. It's about experiencing those little wins, those moments of realization that, "Hey, this really works!" These victories, as small as they may seem, are incredibly powerful. They build your confidence and understanding of the Law of Attraction.

Once you start seeing results, no matter how small, your belief in your ability to manifest grows. It's like a snowball effect; the more you experience success, the more you believe in your capability to achieve even bigger dreams. You'll learn to trust the process and your role in it.

This approach doesn't mean you're giving up on your big dreams. On the contrary, you're preparing yourself for them. You're learning how to align your energy, focus your intentions, and understand the universe's signals. This foundation is crucial for tackling bigger dreams later on.

So, start with something small. Manifest that coffee you've been craving, a great parking spot, or a productive day. Celebrate these successes, and observe how they came into being. Each success story, no matter how small, is a step towards bigger and more complex manifestations. Remember, every big dream starts with a single, smaller step.

9. The Balance of Detachment and Inspired Action

A common stumbling block in the journey of manifestation is not understanding the delicate balance between detachment from outcomes and taking inspired action. Both elements are essential, yet their misalignment can create challenges in manifesting your desires effectively.

- **Detachment from the Outcome:** Detachment is often misunderstood. It doesn't mean not caring about your goal or being indifferent. Rather, it's about not being fixated on a specific outcome or time frame. This fixation can create a sense of desperation or 'death grip' on your desire, which can actually repel what you're trying to attract. It's about having faith that your desires will materialize, but being open to the form they might take. For instance, if you're looking to manifest a new job, detachment means putting your best foot forward in applications and interviews, but not obsessing over every response or opportunity. It's trusting that the right job will come to you, at the right time.

- **Taking Inspired Action:** This is the proactive side of manifesting. It requires you to take real, practical steps towards your goals. However, it's crucial that these actions come from a place of inspiration and alignment with your desires, rather than from fear or a sense of obligation. Inspired action might involve networking for the job seeker, but it should feel like a natural step forward, not a forced effort.

The challenge arises when there's a disconnect between these two aspects. If you're too detached, you might become passive, waiting for things to happen without putting in the necessary effort. On the other hand, without proper detachment, you might find yourself hustling endlessly, fueled by anxiety rather than true desire.

The art of manifesting lies in finding the sweet spot between these two. It's about putting in the effort and then letting go, allowing the universe to work its magic. It's akin to planting a seed: you need to nurture it, but you also need to give it space to grow. Too much interference, like constantly digging it up to check for growth, can hinder its development.

05.

Advanced Manifesting Concepts

Master the Art

1. Manifesting from abundance rather than scarcity

In the realm of advanced manifesting concepts, a pivotal shift occurs when we move from a mindset of scarcity to one of abundance. This shift is not just about changing thoughts; it's about deeply transforming your perspective on life and your role in the universe.

Understanding Scarcity Mindset: Scarcity mindset roots itself in the belief that there isn't enough to go around, that success is limited, and that if someone else wins, you lose. It's a competitive, often fearful view of the world, where you might feel like you have to scramble for your share before it runs out. This mindset can be deeply ingrained, often stemming from past experiences or societal narratives.

The Power of Abundance Mindset: In contrast, an abundance mindset is founded on the belief that there's more than enough for everyone. It views success, happiness, and fulfillment as unlimited resources that can be shared and multiplied. From this perspective, the success of others isn't a threat but a confirmation of the limitless possibilities that exist. It's a collaborative and expansive way of thinking and being.

Shifting from Scarcity to Abundance: The shift from scarcity to abundance is not just about positive thinking; it's about a fundamental change in your belief system. It involves recognizing and challenging the deep-seated beliefs that underpin the scarcity mindset.

This shift can be facilitated through various practices:

- **Reflect and Acknowledge:** Take time to reflect on areas of your life where you feel scarcity. Acknowledging these feelings is the first step towards change.
- **Cultivate Gratitude:** Gratitude is a powerful tool for shifting perspective. By focusing on what you have, rather than what you lack, you open yourself to experiencing more joy and fulfillment.
- **Celebrate Others' Success:** Instead of feeling threatened or envious, celebrate the achievements of others. This practice reinforces the belief in abundance and the joy of shared success.
- **Visualize Abundance:** Visualization exercises can be powerful in shifting your mindset. Imagine a world where there is enough for everyone, your needs are easily met, where opportunities are plentiful, and where you can achieve your dreams without limitation.
- **Adopt an Expansive View:** Look at life through a lens of possibility rather than limitation. Believe in your own potential and the universe's capacity to provide.

Manifesting from an abundance mindset involves more than just attracting what you want; it's about changing the way you see the world. It's a richer, more fulfilling way to live, not just for yourself but for the collective. As you embrace this new perspective, you'll find that the universe responds in kind, opening doors and creating opportunities that resonate with this expansive way of being.

2. The balance between desire, detachment, and belief

Mastering the art of manifesting involves striking a delicate balance between desire, detachment, and belief. Each of these elements plays a critical role, and understanding how they interconnect can elevate your manifesting journey to new heights.

- **Intense Desire – The Fuel of Manifestation:** Desire is the starting point. It's the deep longing or aspiration that propels you forward. But it's essential to understand that desire in manifesting isn't just about wanting something; it's about aligning that want with your deeper values and vision for your life. Your desires should resonate with the core of who you are, acting as a powerful motivator that drives you towards your goals.
- **Detachment – The Art of Letting Go:** Detachment, often misunderstood, is a vital component of manifesting. As mentioned in the previous parts of this journal, detachment doesn't mean not caring about the outcome; instead, it's about not being overly attached to how and when your desires will manifest. This aspect of detachment is about trusting the process and knowing that what you seek is on its way, or something even

better is aligning for you. It's about maintaining a healthy balance between taking inspired action and allowing the universe to orchestrate the perfect timing and ways for your desires to materialize.

- **Belief – The Anchor of Manifestation:** Belief is what ties desire and detachment together. It's the unwavering trust and confidence in the process of manifesting, in the power of the universe, and most importantly, in yourself. Your belief needs to be strong enough to hold your desire and support your detachment. It's the foundation that sustains your vision through the highs and lows, the certainty that what you seek is not only possible but is already on its way to you.

Creating a Synergistic Balance:

1. **Align Your Desires with Your True Self:** Ensure your desires are a true reflection of your inner values and not just influenced by external factors or fleeting emotions.

2. **Practice Mindful Detachment:** Engage in activities that foster a state of flow and present-moment awareness. This practice helps in letting go of the anxiety and urgency often associated with achieving our goals.

3. **Cultivate Unwavering Belief:** Regularly affirm your beliefs through visualization, affirmations, and other reinforcing activities. Surround yourself with reminders of your belief in the universe's abundance and your ability to manifest.

4. **Embrace Flexibility:** Be open to the idea that the universe might have a plan better than yours. Flexibility in your approach allows for unforeseen, yet potentially more fulfilling, outcomes to emerge.

In advanced manifesting, these three elements—desire, detachment, and belief—work together harmoniously. Desire sets the direction, detachment smooths the path, and belief ensures that you stay the course. Balancing these elements not only enhances your ability to manifest effectively but also brings a sense of peace and fulfillment throughout the journey.

3. Adapting Goals to Present Desires and Coherence

The journey of manifesting is dynamic and ever-evolving, reflecting the changes within us as we grow and develop. It's essential to periodically reassess our goals and dreams to ensure they are still in harmony with our current desires and true self. This process of adjustment encourages us to stay authentic and aligned with our genuine aspirations.

Aligning with the Now:

- **Present Alignment:** Evaluate if your current goals resonate with who you are at this moment. Ask yourself, "Is this dream reflective of my current values and aspirations, or does it belong to a past version of myself?"
- **Immediate Reality vs. Distant Future:** Sometimes, we set goals for a distant future without considering if they align with our immediate reality or desires. Reflect on whether your goals are

something you truly desire in your present life or if they are aspirations for a far-off future that may never align with your evolving self.

- **Discerning True Desires from External Influences:** It's crucial to distinguish between what is genuinely your desire and what might be an expectation imposed by family, society, or past influences. This discernment involves deep introspection to understand if your dream is truly yours or if it's shaped by external factors.
- **Letting Go of Outdated Dreams:** Holding onto dreams that no longer serve you can be limiting. If you had a childhood dream of becoming an NBA basketball player but are now 40 and have never played professionally, it might be time to let that specific dream go. Acknowledge the shift in your interests and passions, and give yourself permission to dream anew.
- **Feeling into Your True Desires:** Connect with your inner self and feel into what truly excites and motivates you now. This connection might reveal new dreams and aspirations that are more aligned with your current state of being.

Steps for Adjusting Goals:

1. **Reflect and Reevaluate:** Regularly take time to reflect on your goals. Ask yourself if they still bring excitement and if they align with your current life path.

2. **Be Open to Change:** Embrace the fluidity of life and be open to modifying your goals as you grow. Life is a journey of discovery, and your dreams should evolve with you.

3. **Connect with Your Inner Self:** Engage in practices like meditation, journaling, or quiet contemplation to connect with your innermost desires and understand what truly matters to you now.

4. **Release with Gratitude:** If you decide to let go of a dream, do so with gratitude. Acknowledge the role it played in your life and the lessons it taught you.

5. **Embrace New Aspirations:** Allow yourself to dream new dreams. Be curious about what excites you now and explore these new interests with enthusiasm.

Remember, manifesting is not just about achieving set goals; it's about the journey towards realizing your true self and living a life that resonates with your deepest desires. Adjusting your goals to align with your current self is a powerful way to ensure that your manifesting journey remains authentic and fulfilling.

4. Understanding Continuous Manifestation

The concept of continuous manifestation is a pivotal understanding in the journey of self-realization and the practice of the Law of Attraction. It's the awareness that we are always in a state of creating and manifesting, influenced by our thoughts, emotions, and beliefs, whether consciously or subconsciously.

The Incessant Nature of Manifestation:

- **Unceasing Creation:** Manifestation doesn't pause or stop; it's a continuous process. Our thoughts and feelings are constantly sending signals to the universe, which in turn responds by shaping our experiences and reality.
- **The Power of Thought:** Our thoughts, both positive and negative, have a profound impact on what we attract into our lives. This principle is evident when we reflect on past experiences where our fears and worries seemingly brought about the very circumstances we hoped to avoid.
- **The Universe's Response:** The universe doesn't discriminate between what we want and what we don't want. It simply responds to the vibrational energy we emit. If our dominant thoughts are tinged with fear, doubt, or negativity, the universe aligns our experiences accordingly.

Embracing and Directing Continuous Manifestation:

- **Mindfulness of Thoughts:** Being mindful of our thoughts is crucial. Regularly check in with yourself to observe what you're thinking and feeling. Are your thoughts predominantly positive and hopeful, or are they laden with worry and pessimism?
- **Shifting the Focus:** If you find yourself dwelling on negative outcomes, consciously shift your focus to more positive or neutral thoughts. This doesn't mean ignoring your fears but acknowledging them and then choosing to focus on thoughts that serve you better.

- **Understanding Emotional Guidance:** Your emotions are a powerful guide in understanding your alignment with your desires. Feelings of joy, excitement, and love indicate alignment, whereas feelings of fear, anger, or sadness can signal misalignment and the need to adjust your focus.
- **Learning from the Past:** Reflect on instances where your fears materialized. Use these as learning experiences to understand the power of your thoughts and the importance of maintaining a positive outlook.
- **Cultivating Positive Expectation:** Practice expecting positive outcomes. This doesn't mean being overly optimistic but rather holding a general belief that things will work out in your favor.
- **Integrating Positive Affirmations:** Use affirmations to reinforce positive beliefs and expectations. Repeat statements that affirm your ability to manifest your desires and trust in the benevolent nature of the universe.

Remember, you are a powerful creator, and your thoughts and emotions are the tools with which you sculpt your reality. By understanding and embracing the concept of continuous manifestation, you can more effectively direct your creative powers to manifest a life that reflects your truest desires and aspirations.

5. Manifesting Without Backup Plans

When it comes to manifesting your deepest desires, the concept of going "all in" is crucial. This means letting go of the safety nets and backup plans that, while offering comfort, might actually hinder your manifestation journey. It's a bold step, requiring not just faith in the Law of Attraction but also immense trust in yourself.

The Underlying Challenge with Backup Plans:

Having a backup plan is often seen as a practical approach to life's uncertainties. However, in the realm of manifestation, it can be a subtle indicator of doubt. Holding onto a plan B suggests that somewhere, deep down, you might not fully believe in the possibility of your dream coming true. This split focus can send confusing signals to the universe. Manifestation thrives on clarity and conviction, and a backup plan might dilute the intensity of your intentions.

Fully Investing in Your Dreams:

1. **Wholehearted Belief:** The first step is to nurture a deep, unwavering belief in your dream. This means aligning your thoughts, feelings, and actions with the conviction that what you desire is not only possible but is also on its way to you.

2. **Letting Go of Doubts:** Doubts can creep in subtly, often disguised as practicality or rationality. Recognize these doubts for what they are – barriers to your manifestation process. Letting go of them involves an internal shift, a decision to trust the process and your capabilities fully.

3. **Energetic Alignment:** Your energy and focus should be entirely aligned with your desired outcome. This alignment is more than just thinking positively; it's about feeling and living as if your dream is already in motion. It's a state where every action and thought reinforces your commitment to your goal.

4. **Embracing Uncertainty:** Part of committing fully to your dream involves being comfortable with uncertainty. It's about understanding that not having a backup doesn't mean you're unprepared; it means you're confidently open to the way your desire will manifest, even if it's not in the way you initially imagined.

5. **Visualizing with Conviction:** Visualization is a powerful tool in the Law of Attraction. When you visualize, immerse yourself completely in the experience of your dream coming true. Feel the emotions, embrace the sensations, and live in that moment of achievement, reinforcing your commitment to your goal.

6. **Overcoming the 'What Ifs':** The 'what if it doesn't work out' thoughts can be persistent. Acknowledge these thoughts, thank them for trying to protect you, and then gently let them go. Replace them with affirmations that reinforce your trust in the universe and your own manifesting power.

Taking this leap, where you fully commit to your dream without a safety net, is a testament to your faith in the Law of Attraction and your own co-creative power. It's an empowering stance, one that declares your readiness to receive what the universe has in store for you. Remember, it's not about recklessness; it's about informed, conscious trust and commitment to your path of manifestation. This unwavering focus and dedication can be the key that unlocks doors to your desired reality, transforming your dreams from mere thoughts into tangible experiences.

6. The Essence of Good Intentions in Manifesting

As we delve deeper into manifesting, it's crucial to address the core from which all your manifestations should spring - good intentions. The intention behind your desires significantly influences the energy you put out into the universe and, consequently, what you attract back into your life.

Your journey with this journal began with a clear intent - to harness the Law of Attraction for positive transformation. This foundation is not just a guiding principle for the journal but also a reflection of how your manifestations should be rooted.

1. **Good Intentions as a Guiding Force:** The intentions behind your goals and desires act as a guiding force. They shape not only the outcome but also the journey towards achieving those outcomes. When your intentions are grounded in positivity, generosity, and a desire for growth, they set a powerful and constructive tone for your manifestation journey.

2. **Impact on Personal Energy:** Good intentions have a profound impact on your personal energy. They keep your mind and heart in a place of integrity and alignment with your core values. This alignment is crucial in attracting experiences and opportunities that resonate with those values.

3. **Manifesting for the Greater Good:** When your intentions are focused not just on personal gain but also on contributing positively to the world around you, your manifesting process takes on a deeper, more meaningful dimension. It becomes a tool for

not only personal fulfillment but also for contributing to the well-being of others.

4. **Avoiding Selfish Motives:** Manifesting with good intentions means steering clear of selfish or harmful motives. It's about ensuring that your desires don't come at the expense of others or from a place of negativity or harm.
5. **The Ripple Effect of Positive Intentions:** Good intentions in manifesting create a ripple effect. They influence not only your life but also the lives of those around you. By focusing on positive intentions, you contribute to a collective energy of positivity and abundance.

06.

Practical Tips for Effective Manifesting

Daily Tangible Practices

Welcome to the practical aspect of your manifestation journey. While understanding the concepts and theories behind the Law of Attraction is essential, it's the daily, tangible practices that turn these ideas into reality. This chapter is dedicated to provide you with concrete, actionable steps you can incorporate into your daily routine to enhance your manifesting abilities. It's about turning the abstract into the actual, ensuring that your dreams don't just stay dreams but evolve into reality.

1. The power of gratitude

Gratitude is more than just saying 'thank you.' It's a profound practice that reshapes how you view the world, shifting your focus from what's missing to the abundance that's already present in your life. This shift is vital in the Law of Attraction, as it aligns your energy with abundance, making you more receptive to the universe's gifts.

- **A Shift in Focus:** Regular gratitude practice turns your attention to the positive aspects of your life, no matter how small. This shift in focus is critical in manifesting, as it moves you away from a mindset of lack and into one of abundance.

- **Simple Yet Profound:** The beauty of gratitude lies in its simplicity. It doesn't require grand gestures or elaborate rituals. It's about acknowledging and appreciating the everyday blessings – the morning coffee, a helpful colleague, a beautiful sunset.

- **Daily Practice:** To truly harness the power of gratitude, make it a daily practice. Whether it's writing it down, mental acknowledgments, or verbal expressions, find a way that resonates with you to consistently acknowledge the good in your life.

- **Cultivating an Abundance Mindset:** As you practice gratitude, you'll notice a gradual yet profound change in your overall outlook. You'll start perceiving the world as a place of abundance rather than scarcity. This mindset is crucial in attracting more abundance and joy into your life.

- **Amplifying Positive Energy:** Gratitude amplifies positive energy within and around you. It's an emotional and energetic 'thank you' to the universe, which, in turn, responds with more positive experiences.

- **Simple Start:** Begin with something as simple as writing three things you're grateful for each morning. These could be experiences, people, or even challenges that have brought growth and learning.

In recognition of gratitude's immense power, we have integrated it into the daily practice of this journal. Each page offers a space to record what you're grateful for, encouraging you to make gratitude a natural part of your manifestation journey. This consistent practice serves as a reminder of the abundance already present in your life, setting a foundation for attracting even more.

2. Detaching from Specific Outcomes

In the journey of manifesting, learning to detach from specific outcomes is as vital as setting your intentions. Let's explore some techniques to master this art of detachment.

- **Cultivating an Open Mind:** The first step in detaching from specific outcomes is to cultivate an open mind. This involves accepting that the universe might have a different, perhaps better, plan for achieving your desires than what you have envisioned. For instance, if you're manifesting a new job, be open to opportunities that may not exactly match your expectations but could potentially be more rewarding.
- **Living in the Present Moment:** Focusing on the present moment is a powerful way to detach. It involves immersing yourself in the here and now, rather than obsessing over future outcomes. Engaging fully in your current activities, whether work, hobbies, or spending time with loved ones, helps shift your focus away from anxieties about future results.
- **Trust the Process:** Developing trust in the process of manifesting is key to detaching from specific outcomes. It's about

believing that the universe will guide you to what's best for you, even if it doesn't align with your initial plan. Think of the times when unexpected twists led to positive outcomes you hadn't anticipated.

- **Visualize the Feeling, Not Just the Outcome:** When visualizing your dreams, focus more on the feelings they evoke rather than the exact specifics. For example, if you're manifesting a new home, instead of fixating on the number of rooms or location, focus on the sense of security, comfort, and happiness you anticipate from living in your new space.

- **Mindfulness and Meditation:** Mindfulness and meditation are effective tools for detaching. They help calm the mind and reduce attachment to specific outcomes by bringing your focus back to your internal state and the present moment.

- **Journaling:** Journaling can also be an effective way to process and release your attachment to outcomes. Write about your desires, but also express your willingness to accept whatever the universe has in store for you.

- **Celebrate Small Wins:** Acknowledging and celebrating small achievements along the way can shift your focus from the end goal to the journey itself. It helps you see the value in every step of the process, reducing the pressure on the final outcome.

- **Embrace Uncertainty:** Learning to be comfortable with uncertainty is a part of detaching from specific outcomes. Recognize that uncertainty is a natural part of life and that being too rigid in your expectations can limit your experiences and opportunities.

- **Letting Go Rituals:** Engage in personal rituals that symbolize letting go. This could be as simple as writing down your desires on paper and then burning it, symbolizing your release of attachment to them.

In essence, detaching from specific outcomes is about embracing flexibility, living in the present, and trusting that the universe will deliver what is best for you. It's a balance between intention and surrender – setting your sights on what you desire while being open to the journey and the destination that life has in store for you.

3. Inspired Action: Creating Opportunities for Manifestation

Taking inspired action is a crucial step. It's about creating opportunities for your dreams to become reality. This concept goes beyond mere wishful thinking or passive waiting. Let's delve into how inspired action can be effectively integrated into your manifestation practice.

Inspired action is about aligning your actions with your intentions. It means taking steps that feel naturally driven by your inner desires and intuition, rather than forced or purely logical decisions. For instance, if you're manifesting a new career path, inspired action might involve networking, acquiring new skills, or even spontaneously reaching out to someone who can offer guidance or opportunities.

Your intuition often guides you towards actions that align with your manifestation goals. It could be a sudden urge to attend a particular event, start a new project, or reach out to someone. Trusting these intuitive nudges and acting upon them can open doors that you might not have anticipated.

Inspired action is not about overexertion or straining to make things happen. It's about finding the balance between making efforts and allowing things to unfold naturally. This means doing your part but not forcing outcomes or becoming overly attached to a specific path or timeline.

Stay open to opportunities, even if they appear in unexpected forms or come from unforeseen directions. Sometimes, what starts as a small, unrelated step can lead to significant breakthroughs in manifesting your desires.

To act inspiredly, you need to have clear intentions. Know what you want to manifest and why. This clarity will guide your actions and help you recognize opportunities that align with your goals.

Remember, inspired action doesn't always have to be grand or dramatic. It can be as simple as making a phone call, sending an email, or joining a group that resonates with your goals. These small steps can create a momentum that leads to bigger changes.

Often, taking the first step requires overcoming fear and doubt. Remind yourself that each action you take is moving you closer to your goals, even if the path isn't always clear.

Ensure that your actions align with your core values and the essence of what you wish to manifest. This alignment creates a powerful synergy between your intentions and your efforts.

Regularly reflect on the actions you've taken. Ask yourself if they feel right and are leading you towards your goals. Be prepared to adjust your course as necessary, staying flexible and responsive to your journey.

Incorporating inspired action into your manifestation process is about harmonizing intention with effort. It's recognizing that while setting intentions is crucial, it's the steps you take towards those intentions that bring them to life. Inspired action is the bridge between the world of thought and the world of tangible results. By tuning into your intuition, aligning your actions with your goals, and staying open to opportunities, you actively participate in the co-creation of your reality.

07.

Setting Your Manifestation Goals

Sculpting Your Reality

Welcome to a transformative moment in your journey with this journal. You're at a crossroads where learning turns into doing. It's time to take the wisdom you've absorbed and shape it into real, achievable goals. This isn't just about writing down future dreams; it's about bringing them into your present life. Each goal is a bridge between your current life and the one you dream of, actively integrating your deepest desires into your reality today.

1. Setting the Stage for Your Goals

Embarking on this journey of setting your goals, you're not just charting a course for the future; you're actively sculpting your reality. This crucial step in your manifestation journey is about more than just penning down aspirations; it's about aligning your desires with your truest self, making them a vivid part of your present existence.

Imagine you're at a crossroads where one path represents your current life and another, the life you dream of. It's here that you have the power to choose your direction. This is where the magic happens. Setting your goals is like drawing a map from one point to the other, with each goal a landmark guiding you closer to your dream life.

Clarity is Your Compass:

The first and most vital step is gaining clarity. It might seem daunting, like peering through a foggy window, but remember, clarity is a journey, not a destination. Ask yourself, **"What do I genuinely want?"** This isn't about what society expects of you or what your past self might have wanted. It's about what lights up your heart here and now.For instance, if your goal is to start a health and wellness blog, clarify what topics you'll cover, who your target audience is, and what unique perspective you'll bring. This specificity turns a vague aspiration into a tangible plan.

Consider this journal a confidant, a safe space to express your deepest yearnings without fear or judgment. Let your goals be a true reflection of your innermost desires, not tainted by external influences or fleeting whims.

As you jot down your goals, do it in the present tense. Why? Because it bridges the gap between dreaming and living. Instead of saying, "I will find love," affirm, "I am in a loving, fulfilling relationship." Feel the difference? It's about embracing your desires as existing realities, not distant dreams. This subtle shift in language empowers you, turning passive longing into active living.

Your goals should resonate with who you are. They should feel like the missing pieces of your puzzle, fitting seamlessly into the bigger picture of your life. They're not just castles in the air; they're the foundations of the life you're building. For instance, if you've always been passionate about art, your goal might be, "I am creating and sharing my art with the world." It's specific, it's real, and it aligns with your innate talents and passions.

Tackling the Intimidation of Big Dreams:

It's natural to feel overwhelmed by big dreams. But remember, even the grandest castles were built brick by brick. Start with smaller, attainable goals that lead to your larger vision. This helps build confidence and momentum. If your dream is to run a marathon, start with, "I am running a little further each day." It's about taking those first steps and celebrating each stride towards your bigger goal.

Embracing Authenticity in Your Aspirations:

Your goals must be your own. This is your story, your script. Don't let it be ghostwritten by someone else's expectations or societal norms. This is about what makes you come alive, what gives your life purpose and joy. It's not about chasing someone else's dream; it's about realizing your own.

As you embark on this goal-setting journey, remember, it's about bringing your dreams into your now. It's a declaration of faith in yourself and your abilities to shape your world. So, take this step with confidence and clarity. Your goals are not just wishes; they're commitments to yourself, promises of the incredible life that awaits you. Let each goal be a stepping stone towards that life, a life where dreams are not just envisioned but lived.

2. The Language of Manifestation

The power of language in the art of manifestation cannot be overstated. Words are not just a means of communication; they are tools that shape our reality, thoughts, and experiences. In the journey of manifesting your dreams, the way you articulate your goals plays a pivotal role.

Words as Seeds of Intent:

Consider each word you write or speak as a seed that you plant in the garden of the universe. When you articulate your goals, you are planting these seeds. The universe, in response, nurtures these seeds, helping them to grow and flourish. This is why it's crucial to choose words that align with the essence of what you truly desire.

For instance, saying, "I am free from debt" focuses on the concept of debt. Instead, reframe it as, "I am financially abundant and secure." This subtle shift redirects your focus from lack to abundance.

Present Tense, Present Power:

Manifesting is about living in the 'now', not the 'someday'. When you set your goals in the present tense, you're not just hoping for a future outcome; you're affirming that it's already a part of your reality. This present tense language fosters a mindset where you're not chasing your dreams; you're living them. For example, if you're aspiring to become more confident in public speaking, affirm 'I speak confidently and clearly in public settings' rather than 'I will become a good public speaker.

Instead of "I will travel the world," affirm "Each day I am exploring new cultures and experiencing the beauty of the world." This approach transforms your goals from future aspirations into current realities.

Clarity and Specificity: The Clearer, the Closer:

Vague goals can lead to vague outcomes. The universe responds best to clarity and specificity. When you are specific with your language, you provide a clear direction for your energy to flow towards. It's like giving the universe a blueprint of exactly what you desire.

If your goal is to enhance your career, rather than stating, "I want a better job," specify what 'better' means for you. Is it more creative freedom, a leadership role, better work-life balance? The more detailed your description, the more tangible your goal becomes.

Emotional Resonance in Language:

Your words should not only describe your goal but also evoke the feelings associated with achieving it. This emotional resonance amplifies the energy of your intentions. When you write or speak your goals, imbue them with the emotions you anticipate feeling once they are realized. For example, instead of saying, "I am successful," enhance it with, "I am feeling empowered and fulfilled in my successful career."

Language as a Reflection of Belief:

Finally, the language you use reflects your belief in the possibility of your dreams. Doubtful language creates a barrier to manifestation. Affirm your goals with conviction and confidence. Believe in their possibility, and let your language be a mirror of this belief.

Reflecting Belief Through Language:

The words you choose should reflect an unwavering belief in the possibility of your dreams. Language tinged with doubt creates a barrier to manifestation. Speak and write your goals with confidence and conviction, as if they are already unfolding. This belief-infused language is a potent signal to the universe, aligning your vibrations with your desires.

As you articulate your goals, let your words paint a vivid picture of your desired reality. Remember, each word is a brushstroke in the masterpiece of your life. Write and speak with intention, clarity, and belief, and watch as your dreams begin to take shape in the canvas of your reality.

Dealing with Contradictory Intentions:

Make sure your goals are coherent and don't contradict each other. Goals that are at odds can create internal conflict and hinder your manifesting process. Align your aspirations in a way that they support and enhance each other, creating a unified direction for your energy and efforts.

Imagine you have two primary goals: one is to advance in your career, which requires significant time, energy, and maybe even relocation. Your other goal is to spend more quality time with your family, nurturing those relationships. If pursued without a coherent plan, these goals can contradict each other. Focusing intensely on career advancement might mean longer hours at work, frequent travel, or moving to a new city, which could significantly reduce the time you can spend with your family. On the other hand, prioritizing family time might limit your availability for career opportunities that require extensive commitment.

In this scenario, the conflict arises because each goal demands a substantial share of your time and energy, and fulfilling one might come at the expense of the other. To align these goals coherently, you might need to find a balance, such as seeking career opportunities that allow for a flexible schedule or remote work, or involving your family in decisions about relocation and career changes. This way, you can progress in your career while also being present for your family, ensuring that your goals support and enhance each other rather than being in conflict.

3. Realistic Yet Aspirational Balance

In the dance of manifesting, striking a balance between being realistic and aspirational is key. This balance involves setting goals that are grounded in possibility while still stretching the boundaries of your aspirations. It's about recognizing the fine line between dreams that inspire growth and those that may lead to disillusionment due to their improbability.

Your dreams should be ambitious enough to challenge you, yet anchored in a realm where you genuinely believe they can materialize. Here, we tread the path of 'possible but not necessarily probable,' balancing dreams with grounded reality. For instance, if your dream is to transition to a new career in graphic design, start by taking online courses and building a portfolio, rather than immediately quitting your current job. However, if you are aspiring to be a successful entrepreneur in a field you're passionate about, it is a realistic and achievable dream if you have or are willing to develop the necessary skills and knowledge. However, dreaming of becoming a professional athlete at an advanced age without prior training might fall into the realm of improbability.

Tailor your dreams to your unique situation, skills, and resources. This isn't about downsizing your dreams, but shaping them to fit your current life context. Start with goals that feel achievable and gradually work your way up. If your aspiration is a healthier lifestyle, begin with smaller, manageable steps like incorporating daily exercise before setting your sights on a marathon. This incremental approach builds confidence and keeps you motivated.

Choose goals that not only aim for an external achievement but also foster internal growth. Look for aspirations that push you slightly out of your comfort zone while being achievable. This careful balance ensures you're continuously developing and moving forward, without feeling overwhelmed or disheartened.

Your belief in the possibility of your dreams is the fuel that powers your journey towards them. You need to visualize your success and work towards it with a firm belief that it's within your reach. Dreams that align with your belief system and feel possible – no matter how ambitious – have a higher chance of becoming realities.

While your dreams should be rooted in realism, they should also inspire you to reach higher. They should be a blend of what you know you can achieve and what you hope to achieve. This blend keeps your feet on the ground while allowing your heart to soar towards new heights.

In summary, the balance between realistic and aspirational goals in manifesting is like walking a tightrope between two skyscrapers. It requires focus, determination, and a careful assessment of what's achievable. By setting goals that are both grounded and lofty, you create a pathway to a life that's not only achievable but also deeply fulfilling and aligned with your truest aspirations.

4. Embracing the Goal-Setting Process

When you sit down to write your goals, you're not just plotting a course for the future; you're engaging in a profound conversation with your innermost desires and aspirations. This process should be approached with a sense of reverence and introspection. It's an opportunity to reflect on what truly matters to you, what brings you joy, and what aligns with your core values.

Connecting with Nature or Higher Self:

Before you begin writing your goals, take a moment to connect with nature or your higher self. This could involve a quiet walk in the park, a meditative session, or simply a few moments of deep, mindful breathing. Ask the universe, nature, or your inner wisdom what it desires for you. This connection is vital; it helps you tune into a frequency that transcends everyday distractions and aligns you with a broader vision for your life. Before setting goals, you might meditate in a quiet space, asking yourself, 'What brings me true joy?' This introspection can reveal goals aligned with your deepest desires.

Beyond Just Writing Goals:

As you write each goal, remember that this isn't just about what you want to achieve; it's about who you want to become in the process. Your goals should reflect not just your desires but also the qualities and strengths you want to develop. For example, aspiring to be more compassionate, mindful, or courageous can be just as important as achieving external milestones.

A Transformative Process:

Embrace the dynamic and transformative nature of setting goals. It's a journey of discovery, not just a task to be checked off. Your goals may evolve as you grow, gain new experiences, and develop new insights. This fluidity isn't a sign of indecisiveness; rather, it shows your adaptability and responsiveness to life's changing circumstances. As you progress, some goals might become more relevant, while others might no longer resonate with you. This evolution is a natural part of your growth.

Writing Goals: A Declaration of Intent

When you write your goals, do so with conviction and clarity. They are not just words on paper but declarations of your intentions and commitments. Each goal is a promise to your future self, a manifestation of your dreams into reality. Approach this process with enthusiasm, optimism, and a belief in your capability to bring these aspirations to life.

5. Integrating Your Goals into Everyday Life

Now that we've explored setting and articulating your goals, let's see how you can integrate these into various aspects of your daily life. As you embark on this journey of goal-setting, it's crucial to look at your life holistically. You've just explored how to set meaningful, realistic, and inspiring goals. Now, it's time to apply this understanding to different facets of your life. Let's delve into each area, ensuring a balanced approach that encompasses all aspects of your well-being and aspirations.

- **Career and Professional Development:** Envision your ideal professional scenario. Is it leading a team, innovating in your field, or starting your own business? Let this vision guide your goal-setting. Is it about leadership, a career shift, or entrepreneurship? Set goals that resonate with your professional aspirations. For example, "I am leading a team of creative professionals, driving innovative projects that are celebrated in my industry."

- **Personal Growth and Education:** Whether it's acquiring new skills or indulging in intellectual pursuits, your growth is paramount. Write down what learning means to you. You might say, "I am fluently speaking Spanish, engaging in conversations with native speakers with ease and confidence."

- **Health and Wellbeing:** Your physical and mental health are the base of your life. Set goals that focus on enhancing your overall wellness. A goal might read, "I am living a balanced life, nurturing my body and mind equally." Or a more focused one like "I am completing a 10K run effortlessly, feeling energized and strong, with a consistent exercise routine that I enjoy."

- **Relationships and Social Life:** Think about how you wish to cultivate your relationships and social engagements. Perhaps, "I have a deep, meaningful connection with my best friends and I enjoy our daily conversations on the topics close to my heart."

- **Financial Management:** Financial goals are critical for a secure future. Whether it's saving, investing, or budgeting, clearly define your financial aspirations. For instance, "I am confidently managing my finances towards achieving financial independence." Or "I am saving 30% of my income monthly, effortlessly managing my expenses, and investing wisely for a secure future." If financial independence is your aim, set a specific savings goal, like 'I am saving $500 a month,' and couple it with actionable steps like budgeting and investing in low-risk funds.

- **Leisure and Hobbies:** Remember to include what rejuvenates you. It's essential to have goals related to your passions and hobbies. Something like, "I am painting landscapes every weekend, developing my skills, and preparing for my first art exhibition by the end of the year."
- **Spiritual and Ethical Living:** If this is important to you, include goals that align with your spiritual beliefs and ethical standards. An example could be, "I am living a life that reflects my spiritual values and contributing positively to the world around me."or "I am attending weekly meditation sessions to deepen my spiritual practice and live more mindfully."

Career and Professional Development:

Personal Growth and Education:

Health and Wellbeing:

Relationships and Social Life:

Financial Management:

Leisure and Hobbies:

Spiritual and Ethical Living:

08.

The Art of Visualization

Bringing Your Goals to Life

Now that you've clearly defined your goals, the next empowering step in your manifestation journey is visualization. This technique is more than mere daydreaming; it's an active engagement of your senses and emotions to bring your dreams into reality.

Visualizing Your Goals in Action

Once you've written down your goals in these diverse areas, take a moment each day to visualize them. Picture yourself living these goals, experiencing the joy and fulfillment they bring. This visualization is not just a daydream; it's an active part of making your goals a reality. See yourself succeeding in your career, growing personally, enjoying robust health, and flourishing in relationships. Imagine managing your finances with ease and engaging in hobbies that bring you immense joy. Feel the peace and alignment that comes from living a life true to your spiritual and ethical values.

Remember, these goals are not static; they are dynamic and evolving just as you are. Regularly revisit and adjust them as you grow and your circumstances change. This ongoing process is what keeps your goals alive and relevant.

Now, let your journey of manifesting these goals begin. Embrace each goal with belief and anticipation, knowing that with each step you take, you're drawing closer to the life you envision.

Creative Visualization Techniques:

1. **Dynamic Vision Boards:** Go beyond the traditional vision board. Create an interactive one, where you can add, modify, and play with images and symbols that represent your dreams. This could be a digital board on your computer or a physical one in your workspace.

2. **Shower Thoughts:** Transform your daily shower into a visualization session. Write down your dream, laminate it, and place it where you can see it every day. As the water flows, visualize your dreams flowing into your life.

3. **Audio Visualization:** Record yourself talking about your dreams as if they have already happened. Listen to this recording daily, especially during moments of relaxation. Hearing your own voice affirming your dreams adds a layer of personal trust and belief in the process.

4. **Desktop Dreams:** Set your computer's desktop or phone wallpaper to an image representing your dream. This daily visual cue will keep your goal at the forefront of your mind, subtly reinforcing your visualization practice.

5. **Mind Movies**: Create a short, motivational video or slideshow that includes images and clips of your goals, accompanied by inspiring music. Watching this regularly can help reinforce your visualization.

6. **Visualization Box**: Similar to a vision board, but in a box. Place items, pictures, or notes that represent your goals inside the box. Periodically open the box to review and visualize these goals.

7. **Sensory Immersion**: Engage all your senses in the visualization process. For example, if your goal is to visit Paris, listen to French music, eat French cuisine, and look at pictures of Parisian landmarks while you visualize.

8. **Creative Writing**: Write a story or a detailed journal entry about a day in your life after achieving your goals. This can be a powerful way to clarify and solidify your visions.

9. **Mindful Walking**: Go for a walk and with each step, visualize yourself moving closer to your goals. Use the rhythm of your steps to reinforce a sense of progress and attainment.

10. **Memory Lane Future**: Imagine visiting your future self who has already achieved the goals. Have a conversation with this future version of you, asking for advice or insights about the journey.

The Balance in Details

While details can inspire enthusiasm, avoid getting too fixated on them. The key is to find a balance that excites you without causing attachment to specific outcomes. Repeating the same detailed scenario in your head over and over again can lead to over-attachment, hindering the detachment essential for manifestation.

Practicing Visualization

Visualization is a skill that can be honed over time. If visualizing details doesn't come naturally, focus on the feeling. Even a single aspect or a general sense of your dream is effective. On the other hand, if you find yourself getting lost in the details, take a step back. Allow the broader picture of your dream to guide your visualization without constraining it with rigid details.

Letting Go and Trusting the Process

Crucial to visualization is the art of letting go. Release the urge to control every aspect of how your dream will manifest. Trust in the natural flow of the universe. As you visualize, do it with an open heart, ready to receive your dreams in whatever form they choose to manifest. Your role is not to dictate the journey but to set the intention and let the universe guide the path.

Remember, visualization is more than just seeing; it's about feeling and believing. As you integrate these practices into your daily routine, you're not just imagining a future; you're creating a vibrational blueprint for your dreams to materialize. Embrace this practice with joy, and watch as the collages of your dreams begin to weave themselves into your reality.

Embracing Visualization with Playfulness and Experimentation

As you delve into the world of visualization, remember that this journey is as much about exploration and playfulness as it is about focus and intention. The beauty of visualization lies in its flexibility and the personal touch you bring to it. It's an art form where your imagination is the canvas, and your desires are the colors.

Finding Joy in the Process:

1. **Experiment with Techniques:** Don't hesitate to try different visualization methods. Some people may prefer creating vivid mental images, while others might find solace in verbal affirmations or written descriptions. The key is to discover what resonates with you and brings you the most joy.

2. **Fun and Creativity:** Visualization shouldn't feel like a chore. Make it fun and play with it. Maybe you enjoy drawing or painting your dreams. Perhaps you find joy in crafting a story around your goals. The process should be uplifting and enjoyable, not a rigid routine.

3. **Adapt and Evolve:** Your visualization practice can change and evolve with you. What works today might not feel right tomorrow. Be open to this evolution. The more aligned your visualization practice is with your current state of mind and emotion, the more effective it will be.

4. **Avoiding Force:** It's important not to force visualization. If on certain days the images don't come naturally, don't push it. Sometimes, taking a break can refresh your perspective and bring renewed energy to your practice.

5. **Play with Possibilities:** Use your visualization time to play with different scenarios and outcomes. Imagine various paths to your goal, different ways your dreams could manifest. This openness can often lead to unexpected and fulfilling manifestations.

6. **Personalization:** Tailor your visualization practice to suit your personality. If you love music, maybe create a soundtrack for your

dreams. If you are a tactile person, create a physical representation of your goal that you can touch and interact with.

At the heart of visualization is the combination of belief and enjoyment. When you engage in visualization with a sense of fun and a strong belief in its power, you set the stage for your dreams to manifest in the most joyful and surprising ways. Remember, the universe responds not just to your thoughts and images but also to the vibrational energy of joy and ease you bring to the process. So, let your visualization practice be a playground of possibilities where your dreams take shape in the most delightful ways.

09.

Daily Practice and Weekly Check-In

As we transition from the realm of visualization and theory into the realm of daily practice, it's time to bring those grand dreams into the tangible world of action and manifestation. This journey, exciting as it is, can sometimes feel daunting, especially when comparing the life we currently live with the one we aspire to. This is where the real beauty of our technique shines through.

Understanding the Impact of Fear on Manifestation

As we delve deeper into the practical aspects of manifesting, it's essential to recognize that the journey towards achieving your dreams isn't just about reaching for the stars. It's also about reshaping your mindset and overcoming deeply ingrained fears and limiting beliefs that may hold you back. Here, in this journal, we provide a unique, fun, and effective way to build your manifestation muscle.

Many of us, when confronted with the gap between our current reality and our dreams, experience a sense of fear and inadequacy. It's natural to feel overwhelmed when your dreams seem far-reaching compared to where you stand now. This fear can manifest as a subconscious belief that our dreams are unreachable, leading to a cycle of disappointment and intensified desperation to make things happen. This state of mind, focused on lack and need, actually hinders the manifestation process.

Manifesting as a Joyful Journey

To counter this, our approach in this journal is to treat manifesting as a delightful and playful journey, rather than a desperate action to change your life overnight. It's about finding joy in the process, being at peace with your current life while playfully reaching for your dreams. This shift in perspective is key to transforming manifestation from a process of 'manufearing' – the unintentional manifestation of fears and negative outcomes – to one of joyful creation.

Starting Small: Building Blocks to Big Dreams

In this journal, we encourage you to start small. While it may seem counterintuitive, beginning with manageable, achievable goals is a powerful strategy. It's about laying down the foundation, brick by brick, for the magnificent structure of your dream life.

Every day, you will have the opportunity to manifest something small. This could be as simple as a pleasant interaction, a productive day, or even finding a perfect parking spot. These small victories are incredibly important. They serve as stepping stones, gradually building your confidence and trust in the process of manifestation. Not manifesting a small wish won't ruin your belief system or day. However, witnessing these small manifestations come to fruition builds a pattern of success and reinforces your confidence in your ability to manifest.

This approach is more than just a strategy; it's a healing journey. As you step into the realm of manifesting your dreams, you carry with you a mix of past experiences and ingrained beliefs. Often, these beliefs, particularly those steeped in limitations and past traumas, act as barriers to your deepest desires. That's where the magic of starting small comes in. It serves as a gentle, nurturing workout for your manifestation muscles, allowing you to build strength, resilience, and confidence without the overwhelm.

By embracing the practice of starting with smaller, achievable goals, you are not just setting the stage for bigger achievements; you are also engaging in a process of self-discovery and healing. You're learning to recognize and move past the silent sentinels of your limiting beliefs, replacing them with a newfound sense of possibility and empowerment.

Scaling Up Your Manifestation Goals

As you get comfortable and start observing small manifestations coming to life, you can gradually escalate your goals. This isn't about being reckless but about responsibly expanding your vision as your belief in your manifesting abilities grows. This scaling-up process is vital, ensuring you don't overwhelm yourself with goals that feel too far-fetched from your current standpoint.

Making Manifestation a Fun Daily Practice

Each day, you will engage in the playful practice of writing down a few simple things you'd like to manifest. This approach turns manifestation into a delightful journey, akin to a game where you experiment and explore with curiosity, rather than pressure or desperation. It's about enjoying the process, celebrating small victories, and progressively building toward your larger dreams. By adopting this light-hearted attitude, you not only make the experience enjoyable but also liberate yourself from 'manufearing,' where fear dominates your manifestation efforts. This daily ritual transforms manifesting from a high-stakes challenge into an enjoyable playground of possibilities.

Flexible Goal Setting: Adapting to Your Beliefs

It's essential to establish goals that resonate with your current beliefs and feel attainable within your immediate reality. This approach ensures you're not aiming for targets that seem too distant or improbable at this moment. Choose goals that not only feel achievable and believable now, but also ones that you can envision manifesting today, within the span of a single day. This immediate timeframe reinforces the concept of manifestation as a tangible, daily experience.

Overcoming Blockages with Evidence-Based Confidence

One of the most significant challenges in manifesting is overcoming internal blockages – feelings of unworthiness, fear of failure, or the infamous 'death grip' on our desires. Our daily practice is designed to navigate through these obstacles. By focusing on small, attainable manifestations, we reduce the pressure and the likelihood of these blockages sabotaging our efforts.

As you consistently witness the fruition of these smaller goals, your belief in the process and in yourself will naturally grow. This evidence-based confidence is a game-changer. It empowers you to gradually increase the scale of your goals, transitioning from the modest to the magnificent, but with a foundation of trust and success already established.

Gratitude: The Golden Thread of Manifestation

Embedding gratitude into your daily manifestation routine transforms it from a mere exercise into a powerful catalyst for abundance. Each day, as part of your manifestation practice, you will consciously acknowledge the small yet significant wins and blessings in your life. This could be as simple as being thankful for a positive interaction, a productive day, or even the beauty of your surroundings. By actively recognizing these moments, you're not only appreciating what you have but also tuning your mindset to a frequency of abundance and receptivity. This practice is crucial in shifting your focus from scarcity to abundance, aligning you with the energy of receiving. It reinforces the belief that the universe is abundant and generous, setting a fertile ground for your larger goals to take root and flourish. Remember, gratitude isn't just a feeling; it's an active, daily choice that magnifies your manifesting potential.

Our Unique Approach: Reverse Engineering Your Dreams

Our approach in this journal is somewhat unconventional – instead of starting with the big, audacious dreams, we reverse engineer them. We start at the ground level, building your manifestation muscle with smaller tasks, and gradually work your way up. This method not only makes the process less overwhelming but also more enjoyable and rewarding.

Remember, the key to successful manifesting is not just about the destination but also about the journey. Each small manifestation is a celebration, a testament to your power as a creator. So, let's embark on this daily practice with a heart full of gratitude and a mind open to the endless possibilities that await.

10.

Daily Journal Layout & Instructions

Your Gateway to Manifestation and Abundance

Over the next pages, you'll find a structured yet flexible framework for 'Design your dream day' entries and weekly check-ins. This routine is designed to align your everyday experiences with your broader manifestation goals. The practice is unique, focusing not just on grand aspirations but also on the beauty of small, daily manifestations. This approach aims to gradually build your confidence in the Law of Attraction, ensuring that you're not overwhelmed but rather gently guided towards realizing your dreams.

Each day, you'll engage in a simple yet powerful routine:

Morning Gratitude

- **Cultivate a Positive Start:** Each morning, anchor your thoughts in abundance. Identify and write down three aspects of your life for which you are deeply grateful. These could range from the comfort of your bed to a recent personal achievement. The key is to start your day with an awareness of the abundance that already surrounds you.

- **Deep Emotional Connection:** As you list these blessings, don't just write them down; deeply feel the gratitude. Let this sensation fill your heart and spread through your entire being. Visualize the elements you are thankful for, immersing yourself in the sensation of gratitude. This emotional engagement transforms a simple exercise into a powerful mood-setter for the day.

Example of a 'Morning Gratitude' Journal Entry

Morning Gratitude

1. *I am grateful for the peaceful sleep last night*
2. *I am thankful for the delicious breakfast that energized my morning*
3. *I appreciate the supportive conversation I had with my friend*

Design Your Dream Day

- **Intentional Day Design:** Post gratitude, shift your focus to shaping your day. Write down 3-4 specific, achievable things you want to manifest. These could be as simple as a meaningful conversation or finding a perfect parking spot. The aim is to set intentions that are within reach yet significant enough to influence your day positively.

- **Engage Your Senses in Visualization:** For each of these four manifestations, close your eyes and vividly visualize them happening. Engage all your senses - what do you see, hear, feel, taste, and smell in these scenarios? This multisensory approach anchors your intentions in the present, making them feel real and achievable.

Example of a 'Design Your Dream Day' Journal Entry

Daily Manifestation Reflections

- ☐ *I effortlessly Found a perfect parking spot right in front of my office.*
- ☐ *I received a compliment from my boss on my innovative ideas during the team meeting.*
- ☐ *I bumped into an old friend at the coffee shop, leading to an enjoyable catch-up.*
- ☐ *My favorite lunch spot had a special offer on my preferred meal, making lunchtime particularly satisfying.*

Evening Check-In and Reflections

- **Evening Manifestation Review:** Revisit your morning's manifestations. Next to each, place a tick if it manifested or a cross if it didn't. This process isn't about self-judgment but understanding how your intentions interact with your daily life.
- **Reflect and Grow:** Use your evening reflection to delve into how your day unfolded. Did your actions align with your intentions? How did you adapt to unexpected situations? This is also a moment for self-appreciation. Identify one aspect of yourself or your actions today that you're proud of, whether it's your patience, creativity, or simply a kind gesture.
- **Journaling Your Day's Journey:** The rest of the space is for you to express additional thoughts, insights, or further gratitude. This is your personal space for expression and growth, a place to document your journey and the evolution of your thoughts and feelings.

This daily journaling routine is your pathway to becoming an active participant in creating the life you desire. By starting each day with gratitude and intention and ending with reflection, you're not only manifesting your dreams but also nurturing a deep sense of self-awareness and appreciation.

As you journey through your daily manifestation practices, you'll come across a special checkpoint every seven days: **the Weekly Check-in**. This reflective pause is your opportunity to broaden your perspective, assess your progress, and realign with your bigger vision. In this journal, we emphasize not just on manifesting specific desires but also on recognizing the unexpected joys and surprises that unfold along the way. Your attention and intention have the power to shape your reality, and these check-ins will help you see the broader picture of your manifestation journey.

Example of an 'Evening Check-In and Reflections' Entry

Daily Manifestation Reflections

☑ *I effortlessly Found a perfect parking spot right in front of my office.*

☑ *I received a compliment from my boss on my innovative ideas during the team meeting.*

☒ *I bumped into an old friend at the coffee shop, leading to an enjoyable catch-up.*

☑ *My favorite lunch spot had a special offer on my preferred meal, making lunchtime particularly satisfying..*

Evening Reflections

Today, I felt productive and balanced. I managed my work well and took time for my health and family. I learned that planning and following through brings me a sense of accomplishment and happiness.

Weekly Check-in Questions:

1. Reflecting on Unexpected Magic: This reflection helps you acknowledge the broader effects of shifting your focus towards positivity and manifestation.

- What unexpected positive experiences or surprises did you encounter this week?
- How have these moments reinforced my belief in the power of positive focus and intention?

2. Evaluating Your Vision and Goals: Revisit your bigger vision.

- How are your daily manifestations aligning with this overarching dream?
- Did I achieve the smaller, daily manifestations I set for myself?

These questions guide you to ensure that your daily actions are in harmony with your long-term aspirations.

3. Celebrating Steps Toward My Vision: Celebrating these steps, no matter how small, is crucial in building momentum and confidence.

- What specific actions or changes, both internally and externally, have I made that bring me closer to my vision?

4. Identifying Areas of Resistance: Understanding these areas is key to unlocking greater potential and clearing the path toward your dreams.

- Where might I be holding back or experiencing resistance?

5. Setting Intentions for the Coming Week:

- Based on my reflections, what are my goals for the upcoming week?

- How can these goals propel me closer to my larger vision?

6. Embodying the Ideal Self: Envision the version of yourself that will confidently and effectively move towards your aspirations.

- What qualities or aspects of myself do I need to embrace or develop to effectively pursue my goals in the coming week?

Using the Weekly Check-in:

These check-ins are designed to be introspective and empowering. They're not just about ticking off achievements but about deepening your understanding of yourself and your manifestation process. By regularly pausing to reflect and plan, you are actively participating in shaping the life you desire. Each question is an invitation to explore your inner world and the external steps you're taking to manifest your dreams.

Use this space to be honest, creative, and visionary. Let your reflections guide you, inspire you, and remind you of the incredible journey you're on. Your weekly check-ins are more than just a recap; they are a celebration of growth, a recognition of change, and a catalyst for continuous transformation.

A Message of Inspiration for Your Journey Ahead:

As you embark on the daily practice of designing your dream day and the weekly ritual of reflection, remember that you are on a transformative journey. Each page you turn and each line you write is a step towards a life crafted by your own intentions and desires. This journal is not just a collection of pages; it's a canvas for your dreams, a playground for your imagination, and a sanctuary for your aspirations.

Every morning, when you express gratitude and set your intentions for the day, you're doing more than just planning; you're weaving the fabric of your reality. Your daily manifestations are like seeds that you plant with care and hope. Some will sprout quickly, others might take time, but each one has the potential to grow into something beautiful and fulfilling.

The weekly check-ins are your moments of introspection and celebration. They are not just a review of what has passed but a compass guiding you towards what's ahead. These reflections are a powerful tool in understanding your journey, recognizing your strengths, and identifying areas where you can grow and flourish.

This practice is about enjoying the journey as much as the destination. Celebrate your successes, learn from the setbacks, and always keep your eyes on the horizon of your dreams. Each step forward, no matter how small, is a victory in its own right.

As you move through this journal, keep in mind that you are the architect of your life. Your thoughts, your words, and your actions are the tools with which you build your future. With each manifestation, with every reflection, you are constructing a life that resonates with your deepest desires and highest aspirations.

Approach each day with a heart full of gratitude, a mind open to possibilities, and a spirit ready to embrace the journey. The pages ahead are blank, ready for you to fill them with your dreams and achievements. Go forth with confidence and joy, knowing that you have the power to shape your life in ways that bring you fulfillment, happiness, and peace.

Together, let's embark on this journey of self-discovery and manifestation. Let your heart be light, your intentions clear, and your spirit undaunted. The path to your dreams unfolds before you, one day, one intention, one grateful moment at a time.

Ready to create your magic? Turn the page, and let's begin...

Design Your Dream Day

Morning Gratitude

Daily Manifestation intentions

- [ ]
- [ ]
- [ ]
- [ ]

Evening Reflections

Design Your Dream Day

Morning Gratitude

Daily Manifestation intentions

- [ ]
- [ ]
- [ ]
- [ ]

Evening Reflections

Design Your Dream Day

Morning Gratitude

Daily Manifestation intentions

- [ ]
- [ ]
- [ ]
- [ ]

Evening Reflections

Design Your Dream Day

Morning Gratitude

Daily Manifestation intentions

- [ ]
- [ ]
- [ ]
- [ ]

Evening Reflections

Design Your Dream Day

Morning Gratitude

Daily Manifestation intentions

- ☐
- ☐
- ☐
- ☐

Evening Reflections

Design Your Dream Day

Morning Gratitude

Daily Manifestation intentions

- [ ]
- [ ]
- [ ]
- [ ]

Evening Reflections

Design Your Dream Day

Morning Gratitude

Daily Manifestation intentions

- [ ]
- [ ]
- [ ]
- [ ]

Evening Reflections

WEEKLY CHECK-IN

What unexpected positive experiences or surprises did you encounter this week?

How have these moments reinforced my belief in the power of positive focus and intention?

How are your daily manifestations aligning with this overarching dream?

Did I achieve the smaller, daily manifestations I set for myself?

What specific actions or changes, both internally and externally, have I made that bring me closer to my vision?

Where might I be holding back or experiencing resistance?

Based on my reflections, what are my goals for the upcoming week?

How can these goals propel me closer to my larger vision?

What qualities or aspects of myself do I need to embrace or develop to effectively pursue my goals in the coming week?

Design Your Dream Day

Morning Gratitude

Daily Manifestation intentions

- [ ]
- [ ]
- [ ]
- [ ]

Evening Reflections

Design Your Dream Day

Morning Gratitude

Daily Manifestation intentions

- [ ]
- [ ]
- [ ]
- [ ]

Evening Reflections

Design Your Dream Day

Morning Gratitude

Daily Manifestation intentions

- [ ]
- [ ]
- [ ]
- [ ]

Evening Reflections

Design Your Dream Day

Morning Gratitude

Daily Manifestation intentions

- [ ]
- [ ]
- [ ]
- [ ]

Evening Reflections

Design Your Dream Day

Morning Gratitude

Daily Manifestation intentions

- [ ]
- [ ]
- [ ]
- [ ]

Evening Reflections

Design Your Dream Day

Morning Gratitude

Daily Manifestation intentions

- ☐
- ☐
- ☐
- ☐

Evening Reflections

Design Your Dream Day

Morning Gratitude

Daily Manifestation intentions

- [ ]
- [ ]
- [ ]
- [ ]

Evening Reflections

WEEKLY CHECK-IN

What unexpected positive experiences or surprises did you encounter this week?

How have these moments reinforced my belief in the power of positive focus and intention?

How are your daily manifestations aligning with this overarching dream?

Did I achieve the smaller, daily manifestations I set for myself?

What specific actions or changes, both internally and externally, have I made that bring me closer to my vision?

Where might I be holding back or experiencing resistance?

Based on my reflections, what are my goals for the upcoming week?

How can these goals propel me closer to my larger vision?

What qualities or aspects of myself do I need to embrace or develop to effectively pursue my goals in the coming week?

Design Your Dream Day

Morning Gratitude

Daily Manifestation intentions

- [ ]
- [ ]
- [ ]
- [ ]

Evening Reflections

Design Your Dream Day

Morning Gratitude

Daily Manifestation intentions

- [ ]
- [ ]
- [ ]
- [ ]

Evening Reflections

Design Your Dream Day

Morning Gratitude

Daily Manifestation intentions

- [ ]
- [ ]
- [ ]
- [ ]

Evening Reflections

Design Your Dream Day

Morning Gratitude

Daily Manifestation intentions

- [ ]
- [ ]
- [ ]
- [ ]

Evening Reflections

Design Your Dream Day

Morning Gratitude

Daily Manifestation intentions

- [ ]
- [ ]
- [ ]
- [ ]

Evening Reflections

Design Your Dream Day

Morning Gratitude

Daily Manifestation intentions

- [ ]
- [ ]
- [ ]
- [ ]

Evening Reflections

Design Your Dream Day

Morning Gratitude

Daily Manifestation intentions

- [ ]
- [ ]
- [ ]
- [ ]

Evening Reflections

WEEKLY CHECK-IN

What unexpected positive experiences or surprises did you encounter this week?

How have these moments reinforced my belief in the power of positive focus and intention?

How are your daily manifestations aligning with this overarching dream?

Did I achieve the smaller, daily manifestations I set for myself?

What specific actions or changes, both internally and externally, have I made that bring me closer to my vision?

Where might I be holding back or experiencing resistance?

Based on my reflections, what are my goals for the upcoming week?

How can these goals propel me closer to my larger vision?

What qualities or aspects of myself do I need to embrace or develop to effectively pursue my goals in the coming week?

Design Your Dream Day

Morning Gratitude

Daily Manifestation intentions

- [ ]
- [ ]
- [ ]
- [ ]

Evening Reflections

Design Your Dream Day

Morning Gratitude

Daily Manifestation intentions

- [ ]
- [ ]
- [ ]
- [ ]

Evening Reflections

Design Your Dream Day

Morning Gratitude

Daily Manifestation intentions

- [ ]
- [ ]
- [ ]
- [ ]

Evening Reflections

Design Your Dream Day

Morning Gratitude

Daily Manifestation intentions

- [ ]
- [ ]
- [ ]
- [ ]

Evening Reflections

Design Your Dream Day

Morning Gratitude

Daily Manifestation intentions

- [ ]
- [ ]
- [ ]
- [ ]

Evening Reflections

Design Your Dream Day

Morning Gratitude

Daily Manifestation intentions

- [ ]
- [ ]
- [ ]
- [ ]

Evening Reflections

Design Your Dream Day

Morning Gratitude

Daily Manifestation intentions

- ☐
- ☐
- ☐
- ☐

Evening Reflections

WEEKLY CHECK-IN

What unexpected positive experiences or surprises did you encounter this week?

How have these moments reinforced my belief in the power of positive focus and intention?

How are your daily manifestations aligning with this overarching dream?

Did I achieve the smaller, daily manifestations I set for myself?

What specific actions or changes, both internally and externally, have I made that bring me closer to my vision?

Where might I be holding back or experiencing resistance?

Based on my reflections, what are my goals for the upcoming week?

How can these goals propel me closer to my larger vision?

What qualities or aspects of myself do I need to embrace or develop to effectively pursue my goals in the coming week?

Design Your Dream Day

Morning Gratitude

Daily Manifestation intentions

- ☐
- ☐
- ☐
- ☐

Evening Reflections

Design Your Dream Day

Morning Gratitude

Daily Manifestation intentions

- [ ]
- [ ]
- [ ]
- [ ]

Evening Reflections

Design Your Dream Day

Morning Gratitude

Daily Manifestation intentions

- ☐
- ☐
- ☐
- ☐

Evening Reflections

Design Your Dream Day

Morning Gratitude

Daily Manifestation intentions

- [ ]
- [ ]
- [ ]
- [ ]

Evening Reflections

Design Your Dream Day

Morning Gratitude

Daily Manifestation intentions

- [ ]
- [ ]
- [ ]
- [ ]

Evening Reflections

Design Your Dream Day

Morning Gratitude

Daily Manifestation intentions

☐

☐

☐

☐

Evening Reflections

Design Your Dream Day

Morning Gratitude

Daily Manifestation intentions

- ☐
- ☐
- ☐
- ☐

Evening Reflections

WEEKLY CHECK-IN

What unexpected positive experiences or surprises did you encounter this week?

How have these moments reinforced my belief in the power of positive focus and intention?

How are your daily manifestations aligning with this overarching dream?

Did I achieve the smaller, daily manifestations I set for myself?

What specific actions or changes, both internally and externally, have I made that bring me closer to my vision?

Where might I be holding back or experiencing resistance?

Based on my reflections, what are my goals for the upcoming week?

How can these goals propel me closer to my larger vision?

What qualities or aspects of myself do I need to embrace or develop to effectively pursue my goals in the coming week?

Design Your Dream Day

Morning Gratitude

Daily Manifestation intentions

- [ ]
- [ ]
- [ ]
- [ ]

Evening Reflections

Design Your Dream Day

Morning Gratitude

Daily Manifestation intentions

- [ ]
- [ ]
- [ ]
- [ ]

Evening Reflections

Design Your Dream Day

Morning Gratitude

Daily Manifestation intentions

- [ ]
- [ ]
- [ ]
- [ ]

Evening Reflections

Design Your Dream Day

Morning Gratitude

Daily Manifestation intentions

- [ ]
- [ ]
- [ ]
- [ ]

Evening Reflections

Design Your Dream Day

Morning Gratitude

Daily Manifestation intentions

- [ ]
- [ ]
- [ ]
- [ ]

Evening Reflections

Design Your Dream Day

Morning Gratitude

Daily Manifestation intentions

- [ ]
- [ ]
- [ ]
- [ ]

Evening Reflections

Design Your Dream Day

Morning Gratitude

Daily Manifestation intentions

- [ ]
- [ ]
- [ ]
- [ ]

Evening Reflections

WEEKLY CHECK-IN

What unexpected positive experiences or surprises did you encounter this week?

How have these moments reinforced my belief in the power of positive focus and intention?

How are your daily manifestations aligning with this overarching dream?

Did I achieve the smaller, daily manifestations I set for myself?

What specific actions or changes, both internally and externally, have I made that bring me closer to my vision?

Where might I be holding back or experiencing resistance?

Based on my reflections, what are my goals for the upcoming week?

How can these goals propel me closer to my larger vision?

What qualities or aspects of myself do I need to embrace or develop to effectively pursue my goals in the coming week?

11.

Resources and Further Learning

The path of self-discovery, personal growth, and manifestation is ever-evolving and multifaceted. To support and inspire you further, we've included a selection of exceptional teachers. Each of these thought leaders brings a unique perspective to the table, offering insights and techniques that can deepen your understanding and practice of manifestation and self-growth.

1. Emily Fletcher

- Emily is the brilliant mind behind Ziva Meditation, an innovative blend of mindfulness, meditation, and manifesting techniques. Her method is designed to be both powerful and practical, focusing on reducing stress and unlocking your true potential. Emily's teachings are rooted in the philosophy that you don't have to be a monk to meditate and you don't have to be a hippie to practice mindfulness. She makes these practices accessible and relevant for modern-day life.

- What You'll Gain: By following Emily, you can learn to integrate mindfulness into your daily routine, enhance your focus, and tap into your inner power for personal and professional growth.
- Website: https://zivameditation.com/
- Instagram: @emilystellafletcher / @zivameditation

2. Alyssa Nobriga

- Alyssa is a professional coach who stands at the intersection of traditional psychotherapy and contemporary holistic practices. Her integrative approach is aimed at fostering deep personal transformation and helping individuals navigate the complexities of the mind with greater clarity and self-awareness.
- What You'll Gain: Alyssa's teachings provide valuable insights into how to overcome personal obstacles and cultivate a mindset that supports growth and manifestation.
- Website: https://www.alyssanobriga.com/
- Instagram: @alyssanobriga

3. Niraj Soma Naik

- Niraj, a former pharmacist turned wellness innovator, is the creator of Soma Breath, a therapeutic breathwork system. His method combines ancient breathing practices with modern science to promote holistic health and well-being.
- What You'll Gain: Niraj's approach offers a unique perspective on using breathwork as a tool for healing, stress reduction, and aligning with your manifestation goals.
- Website: Soma Breath

- Instagram: @nirajnaikofficial / @somabreath

4. Jay Shetty

- Jay Shetty, a motivational speaker and former monk, is renowned for his wisdom-filled storytelling and practical advice on living a purposeful life. His podcast, "On Purpose," is a treasure trove of conversations about life, purpose, and mindfulness.
- What You'll Gain: Jay provides motivational insights and actionable steps to help you discover your purpose, enhance your mindfulness practice, and manifest your dreams.
- Website: https://jayshetty.me/
- Instagram: @jayshetty

5. Joe Dispenza

- Dr. Joe Dispenza is a celebrated author and speaker with a focus on neuroscience, neuroplasticity, and epigenetics. His work explores the science behind personal transformation and the incredible potential of the human mind to heal and evolve.
- What You'll Gain: Through his teachings, you can delve into the science of manifestation, understand the power of your thoughts, and learn techniques to transform your mind and reality.
- Website: https://drjoedispenza.com/
- Instagram: @drjoedispenza

Each of these experts offers a wealth of knowledge and practical strategies that can be a catalyst for your growth and manifestation journey. Whether you're seeking to deepen your meditation practice, understand the science behind your thoughts, or find new ways to challenge your limiting beliefs, these resources can guide and inspire you. Embark on this exploration with an open heart and mind, ready to embrace new perspectives and transformative ideas.

12.

Conclusion and Encouragement

As we approach the end of this transformative journey through your journal, it's essential to pause and reflect on the progress you've made and the path that lies ahead. Remember, this journal is not just a collection of exercises and reflections; it's a blueprint for a life filled with purpose, abundance, and fulfillment.

Embrace the Journey with Trust and Patience

- **Persist with Faith**: Trust in the process of manifestation. Your journey might have ups and downs, but each step is a crucial part of your growth. If a particular dream or goal hasn't materialized yet, it doesn't signal failure. Instead, it's an invitation to trust that something even better is aligning for you.

- **Gratitude as Your Guiding Light**: Whenever in doubt or feeling overwhelmed, turn to gratitude. It's the most powerful tool to shift your focus from scarcity to abundance. Recognizing and appreciating what you have sets the stage for receiving even more.

Comfort in the Unknown

- **Embrace Uncertainty**: Your dreams may push you out of your comfort zone into the realm of the unknown. It's natural to feel a bit uneasy about what lies ahead. Remember, visualization is a powerful ally here, helping you live your dream in your mind's eye before it unfolds in reality.
- **The Power of 'Maybe'**: Accept the space of 'maybe' and 'in-between'. Let go of the need for absolute certainty. Life is an ever-changing tapestry, and your ability to adapt and stay open-minded is key to manifesting your desires.

Changing Your Focus

- **From Fear to Faith**: Understand that focusing on what you don't want can inadvertently bring it into your life. Shift your energy to what you desire, coupled with positive emotions, to create a powerful manifesting force.
- **Deserving Your Dreams**: Acknowledge that on some level, you might feel undeserving or fearful of your dreams. Recognize these feelings but don't let them dictate your reality. You are worthy of your desires, just as you are.

Small Steps Lead to Big Leaps

- **Progress, Not Perfection**: Manifestation is not about changing everything overnight. It's about gradual, consistent steps towards your larger vision. Celebrate each small victory and acknowledge your growth along the way.

- **Your Unique Path**: Remember, there is only one version of you, and that version is deserving of all the dreams and aspirations you hold. You don't need to change who you are to manifest your desires; you need to embrace and accept yourself fully.

As you close this chapter and look towards your future, carry with you the lessons, insights, and experiences you've gathered. The journey of manifestation is ongoing, and every day presents a new opportunity to create the life you dream of. Keep your heart open, stay grounded in gratitude, and trust in the abundance that life offers. Here's to a future filled with all the beauty, joy, and fulfillment you deserve.

As you reach the end of this journal, you'll find ten lined pages dedicated to your personal use. These pages are your canvas – a space for you to freely express whatever feels right in the moment. You can use them for jotting down additional notes, reflecting on your journey, recording affirmations, or simply capturing thoughts and ideas as they come to you.

Embrace this space as a tool for continuous growth and self-discovery. Happy manifesting!"

Additional Notes, Reflections, and Affirmations

Additional Notes, Reflections, and Affirmations

Additional Notes, Reflections, and Affirmations

Additional Notes, Reflections, and Affirmations

Additional Notes, Reflections, and Affirmations

Additional Notes, Reflections, and Affirmations

Additional Notes, Reflections, and Affirmations

Additional Notes, Reflections, and Affirmations

Additional Notes, Reflections, and Affirmations

Additional Notes, Reflections, and Affirmations

SCAN ME

Discover More Products from Belffy

Belffy

www.belffybooks.com

Printed in Great Britain
by Amazon

45880656R00116